Controlling the Trade of the Dual-Use Items

A Handbook

P.I.E. Peter Lang

Bruxelles · Bern · Berlin · Frankfurt am Main · New York · Oxford · Wien

Quentin MICHEL, Sylvain PAILE,
Maryna TSUKANOVA, Andrea VISKI

Controlling the Trade of the Dual-Use Items

A Handbook

NON-PROLIFERATION AND SECURITY
No. 9

Éditions scientifiques internationales
Brussels, 2013
1 avenue Maurice, 1050 Brussels, Belgium
info@peterlang.com; www.peterlang.com

ISSN 1377-0608
ISBN 978-2-87574-077-9
D/2013/5678/60

CIP available from the Library of Congress, USA, and the British Library, GB.

Bibliographic information published by "Die Deutsche Nationalbibliothek" "Die Deutsche Nationalbibliothek" lists this publication in the "Deutsche Nationalbibliografie"; detailed bibliographic data is available in the Internet at <http://dnb.de>.

Acknowledgement

The authors would like to thank Emily Nickerson for her precious support.

May this raise new scientific interests and debates.

Contents

What to Control?

How to Control?

Introduction

How to minimise the possibility that the use of weapons of mass destruction (WMD) has challenged civilisation since the first written accounts of war? As far back as the 5th Century B.C., warring factions recognised the utility of certain types of WMD in warfare, insofar as they were able to kill large numbers of people as well as instil fear, panic, and disorganisation. To this day, preventing the spread and use of these weapons remains a priority, especially as globalisation has broadened access to increasingly sophisticated WMD technology by both state and non-state actors.

In this context, the trade of certain types of technology, materials, and equipment captures the difficulty of controlling WMD. Trade spreads capacity, technological development and know-how and can therefore determine whether or not a state or non-state actor will acquire the necessary means to use WMD. In a world where nuclear energy is becoming a common alternative to other forms of energy generation, especially in developing countries, Trade regulations decreasing the risk of WMD proliferation must be a top priority for the international community.

Among many existing tools to stem the spread of WMD, export controls are becoming increasingly important as a way for countries to ensure that they are not contributing to proliferation. While in the past export controls have been defined quite narrowly, usually referring to requirements for a case-by-case review of certain limitations placed on exports of particular items of concern to certain destinations, in the past decade or so the definition has broadened to encompass a variety of measures necessary to effectively control trade so as not to contribute to proliferation. The term "export controls" is plural because there is not one independent export control measure, but rather a set of measures, functioning in unison and aiming at addressing one component of WMD proliferation: the flow of goods that potentially have a WMD application. These are the measures that will be explained in this Handbook, from licencing procedures to the role of industry outreach to other concerns such as intangible technology transfers (ITT). This Handbook will clearly explain the basic elements necessary to implement an effective export control system, particularly with the changing international landscape in mind.

Due to the growing importance of export controls, and especially since the creation of an international legally binding framework, to implement them from United Nations Security Council Resolution 1540 in 2004, there have been discussions regarding moving on from the term "export controls" in order to play down the negative connotations associated with the word "control", as well as to better reflect the wider span of measures related to this instrument. Suggestions have been put forth to replace the term with "management of strategic trade" or "facilitation of responsible exports", to name just a few. The aim of these new terms is to lessen the impression that the term "control" implies, namely that there is one party in control, and another being controlled. In the context of trade, the controller/controlled dichotomy can mean a licencing office and company, an international organisation and its member States, or one country trying to control the exports of another. In addition, the term "export" similarly no longer reflects the variety of measures associated with this term, which pertain to not just export but in some cases transhipment, import, or other activities related to the trade of certain goods. In either context, the term "export control" does not lend justice to the true nature of the measures used to manage nuclear trade, which are much broader and more diverse than the term implies. While adopting a new term to replace "export controls" would be welcome and beneficial to the field, such a term has yet to be agreed upon, accepted, and used widely by the international community.[1] Therefore, for the sake of consistency, clarity, and simplicity, the term "export controls" will be used throughout this handbook.

---

1 Terms like "trade control" or "sensitive trade control" are the most commonly used.

Why Controlling?

The Political Context

This first part of the Handbook explains what WMD are and identifies other definitions crucial to the understanding of export controls. It will also identify the reasons for which export controls are important, with special focus on nuclear energy, nuclear renaissance and the link with nuclear proliferation. The second part of this section will provide an introduction to the term "dual-use" and the evolution of export controls to include goods that can be used for both civilian and WMD purposes.

What is a weapon of mass destruction?

Definition and evolution of the term

The term "weapon of mass destruction" was first used by the Archbishop of Canterbury, Cosmo Gordon Lang, in 1937 following an aerial bombing of the Spanish city of Guernica during the Spanish Civil War. The Archbishop, in a Christmas message, asked:

> Who can think at this present time without a sickening of the heart of the appalling slaughter, the suffering, the manifold misery brought by war to Spain and to China? Who can think without horror of what another widespread war would mean, waged as it would be with all the new weapons of mass destruction?[1]

Of course Lang was not speaking of WMD in the specific context in which the term is used today; nevertheless, the massive destruction brought about by advances in technology as applied to the weapons to which he referred led to the eventual grouping of certain types of weapons into the modern definition of WMD.

It was not until the Cold War and post-Cold War era that the term became exclusively attributed to nuclear, biological and chemical weapons, and increasingly the term is even used for radiological weapons. Perhaps the easiest way to conceptualise what falls under WMD is to differentiate the term from conventional weapons. Conventional weapons commonly refer to items such as small arms and light weapons, sea and land mines, bombs, shells, rockets, missiles, and

---

[1] Cortright, D., Lopez, G. (eds.), *Uniting against terror: Cooperative military responses to the global terrorist threat.* Cambridge, MIT Press, 2007. See also the Archbishop's Appeal, *Times* (London), 28 December 1937, p. 9.

cluster munitions. "WMD" suggests the use of unconventional means, namely chemical, biological and nuclear, to inflict mass casualties. The following section gives a brief overview of the types of weapons referred to in the umbrella term of WMD.

Nuclear weapons

Nuclear weapons have been and are still considered as a symbol of supreme power, not only military but also politically. If nuclear weapons have been used only twice in war conflicts, different nuclear explosive devices have been tested massively and large quantities of nuclear weapons are held by the eight official (the USA, Russia, the United Kingdom, France, China) and unofficial (India, Pakistan, Israel and North Korea) "nuclear weapons" States. This list should be completed by a few suspicious countries, in particular Iran, for which there are grounds to believe that they are engaged in a nuclear weapons research program.

The nuclear weapon is the only weapon of mass destruction for which an international treaty legally recognises the possession: the Treaty on the Non-Proliferation of Nuclear Weapons (NPT). For this treaty, the legal holders are the States that have manufactured and exploded a nuclear weapon or other nuclear explosive device prior to 1st January 1967.[2] In this regard, only the USA, Russia, the United-Kingdom, France, and China have the right to possess nuclear weapons.

There exists two categories of nuclear weapons: the weapons based on the fission process[3] and those based on the fusion process.[4] Both are based on the principle that, in order to sustain a chain reaction, a minimum amount – called the "critical mass" – of fissile material is required. When this amount is assembled in a plain sphere shape, the

---

2 Article IX.3 of the NPT.

3 During the process of nuclear fission a particle such as a neutron strikes the nucleus of a uranium or plutonium atom and causes it to split into two fragments. Each of the two fragments consists of a nucleus with roughly half the neutrons and protons of the original nucleus. This fission process releases a large amount of energy in the form of warmth and radiation. Gamma rays are emitted as well as two or more neutrons that are no longer bound by the fission fragments. These so-called "free" neutrons are now capable of splitting other uranium or plutonium nuclei, which then release neutrons that split still more nuclei. A series of such nuclear fissions is called a "chain reaction", which is accompanied by an enormous release of nuclear energy.

4 Fusion constitutes in the melding of two atoms, which produces extraordinary amounts of energy. Nevertheless, fusion reactions can occur only at many millions of degrees Kelvin when the electrostatic forces of repulsion that result from the presence of positive electric charges in both nuclei can be overcome so that the nuclear forces of attraction can perform a fusion. Such high temperatures, however, do only occur in suns or in uncontrolled nuclear chain reactions (fission bomb).

risk of spontaneous ignition of the chain reaction is high. As to to avoid such event, two types of fission bombs have been tested. The gun-barrel design, which uses conventional explosives, propels a subcritical mass of uranium down a barrel for collision with another subcritical mass. The bomb dropped on Hiroshima was of this type. The empty sphere shape design is an implosion device which uses conventional explosives and reflectors surrounding a subcritical mass of nuclear material. When the explosives are detonated simultaneously, the pressure of the central core is so great that it compresses the material in a plain sphere shape to criticality.

The fusion bomb constitutes of a fission bomb boosted up by a nuclear fusion, which considerably enhances the destructive potential. The fusion reaction is obtained by infusing a mixture of the heavy hydrogen isotopes deuterium and tritium into the fission reaction.

Nuclear weapons are characterised by the fact that their conceptual principles are rather easy to understand but are technically difficult to implement. Nevertheless, the system of the first uranium gravity fission bomb dropped on Hiroshima has not been tested before use. One of the main difficulties lies in the process to produce the necessary fissile material. Compared to chemical and biological weapons, the nuclear weapon has a high level – and not selective – destruction power.[5]

Biological weapons

Throughout history, infectious diseases contracted naturally have had a significant impact on military operations. The intentional dissemination of disease added a new dimension to threats posed by infectious and toxic agents traditionally transmitted only by natural routes. Such agents have been used notably:[6]

- By Japan in 1939 to poison Soviet water supply with intestinal typhoid bacteria at former Mongolian border;
- By Japan in 1940 who dropped rice and wheat mixed plague-carrying fleas over China and Manchuria;
- By Germany in May 1945 to poison a large reservoir in Bohemia with sewage.
- When the United States faced, in autumn 2001, a wave of letters contaminated with anthrax, which killed five people and affected 17 others.

---

5 The bomb dropped on Hiroshima bomb has a yield of 12-15 Kt and the largest nuclear weapon tested was Russian and had a yield of 58 Mt (4296 times larger).

6 All the data come from Centre For Non-Proliferation Studies, Monterey Institute of International Studies. Source: http://cns.miis.edu.

Numerous countries have, in the past, initiated a biological weapons research programme but, presently, countries of concern are rather limited. Since September 2001, concerns have mostly focused on the risk that non-state actors, such as terrorists, could elaborate biological weapons.

Biological weapons are characterised by the fact that they are rather difficult to elaborate and present a high level of instability (preservation conditions are uneasy to maintain). Nevertheless, facilities to elaborate such weapons and the weapon itself are rather easy to hide and in some ways to use. For instance, the toxic agent could be hidden and dispersed through a container looking like a classical perfume bottle.

The ability of biological agents to multiply in the body over time actually increase their effect and distinct them from their chemical counterparts. Biological agents, which may be used as weapons, can be classified as follow:[7]

Bacteria. Bacteria are small free-living organisms, most of which may be grown on solid or liquid culture media. The organisms have a structure consisting of nuclear material, cytoplasm, and cell membrane. They reproduce by simple division. The diseases they produce often respond to specific therapy with antibiotics.

Viruses. Viruses are organisms, which require living cells in which to replicate. They are therefore intimately dependent upon the cells of the host, which they infect. They produce diseases which generally do not respond to antibiotics but which may be responsive to antiviral compounds, of which there are few available, and those that are available are of limited use.

Rickettsiae. Rickettsiae are microorganisms which have characteristics common to both bacteria and viruses. Like bacteria, they possess metabolic enzymes and cell membranes, utilise oxygen, and are susceptible to broad-spectrum antibiotics. They resemble viruses in the measure that they grow only within living cells.

Chlamydia. Chlamydiae are obligatory intracellular parasites incapable of generating their own energy source. Like bacteria, they are responsive to broad-spectrum antibiotics. Like viruses, they require living cells for multiplication.

Fungi. Fungi are primitive plants, which do not utilise photo-synthesis, are capable of anaerobic growth, and draw nutrition from decaying vegetable matter. Most fungi form spores, and free-living

7 This classification comes from the Federation of American Scientists. Source: http://www.fas.org.

forms are found in soil. The spore forms of fungi are operationally significant. Fungal diseases may respond to various antimicrobial.

Toxins. Toxins are poisonous substances produced and derived from living plants, animals, or microorganisms; some toxins may also be produced or altered by chemical means. Toxins may be countered by specific antisera and selected pharmacological agents.

The intrinsic features of biological agents, which influence their potential for use as weapons, include: infectivity, virulence, toxicity, incubation period, transmissibility, lethality and stability.

Of the few types of WMD, biological weapons are the most difficult to detect because their results often do not become apparent until well after an attack. This also makes the original attacker harder to trace.

Chemical weapons

Chemical weapons are charged with a toxic chemical contained in a delivery system such as a bomb or artillery shell. It was used for the first time on 22 April 1915 near Ypres where 6,000 cylinders containing 168 tonnes of chlorine were deployed by two battalions along six kilometres of the battlefront. The cloud of gas was dispersed by the wind and killed 5,000 soldiers. After this test, chemical weapons had been used massively by both belligerents until the end of the war. The death toll raised to 1,300,000 (nearly 100,000 of whom died in combat), while losses caused by other forms of weapons were put at 26,700,000 (6,800,000 of whom died in combat) even if improvements made with gas masks and other means of immediate protection considerably reduced total losses caused by gases – especially mustard gas – employed as a weapon of war. Furthermore, chemical weapons have been used:[8]

- Between 1922 and 1927 by Spain against the Riff rebels in the Spanish Morocco;
- In 1936 by Italy which used mustard gas against Ethiopians during its invasion of Abyssinia;
- Between 1962 and 1970 by the United States, which used tear gas and four types of defoliant, including Agent Orange in Vietnam;
- Between 1963 and 1967 by Egypt which used chemical weapons (phosgene, mustard) against Yemen;

---

8 All the data come from Centre For Non-Proliferation Studies, Monterey Institute of International Studies. Source: http://cns.miis.edu.

- Between 1975 and 1983 by Soviet Union which used Yellow Rain (trichothecene mycotoxins) in Laos and Kampuchea;
- Between 1982 and 1988 by Iraq which used various chemical weapons against Iran and against Kurds;
- In March 1995 by the Aum Shinrikyo sect in Tokyo.

Contrary to conventional and nuclear weapons, the destructive power of chemical weapons is, like biological weapons limited to life and does not affect infrastructure and buildings. It usually left a few residuals after use.

If a chemical weapon was the first WMD used in an arms conflict, it was also the first to be banned by an international convention, the 1925 Geneva Protocol for the Prohibition of the Use in War of Asphyxiating, Poisonous or Others Gases, and of Bacteriological Methods of Warfare. Chemical Weapons are often considered as a third-world country WMD, due to the fact that contrary to other WMD, they do not require costly technology. Most of their components could be obtained rather easily on the international market. Moreover, the military purposes could be easily hidden as peaceful chemical facilities could be diverted to produce toxic chemicals.

Chemical weapons have, like small weapons, a long lifetime and large stockpiles exist all around the world. A non-negligible part of those stockpiles is constituted by chemical weapons abandoned on the battlefield by belligerents at the end of World War I.

The toxic component of a chemical weapon is called the "chemical agent". Based on their mode of action (*i.e.* the route of penetration and their effect on the human body), chemical agents are commonly divided into several categories: choking, blister, blood, nerve and riot control agents.[9]

Choking agents inflict injuries mainly on the respiratory tract. They irritate the nose, throat, and especially the lungs. Victims typically inhale these agents, which cause the alveoli to secrete a constant flow of fluid into the lungs, essentially drowning the victim. Examples of choking agents include: chlorine (Cl), phosgene (PG), diphosgene (DP) and chloropicrin (PS). Choking agents were among the first agents produced in large quantities. During World War I both sides used them extensively. Because they sink into and fill depressions, they were well suited to trench warfare. Their successful use on the battlefield led to

---

[9] Data mentioned below are taken from "Fact Sheet 4: What is a chemical weapon" edited by the Organisation for the Prohibition of Chemical Weapons. Available: http://www.opcw.org/docs/fs4.pdf.

research and development programmes to create even more toxic and effective chemical weapons.

Blister agents, or vesicants, are one of the most common chemical weapons agents. These oily substances act via inhalation and contact with skin. They affect the eyes, respiratory tract, and skin, first as an irritant and then as a cell poison. As the name suggests, blister agents cause large and often life-threatening skin blisters, which looks like severe burns. Examples include sulphur mustard (H, HD), nitrogen mustard (HN), lewisite (L) and phosgene oxide (CX). Mustard agents and lewisite are the best known. Blister agents were first tested in combat in 1917 by Germany and were in several conflicts since, notably in the Iran-Iraq War (1980-1988). They are primarily dispersed in liquid or vapour (aerosol) form and may persist for days. Like phosgene, mustard agents have a delayed effect. Deaths typically only represent a small percentage of the casualties they cause. Exposure to blister agents often results in blindness and permanent damage to the respiratory system.

The name *blood agent*, like those of other groups of agents, derives from its effect on victims. Blood agents are distributed via the blood and generally enter the body via inhalation. They inhibit the ability of blood cells to utilise and transfer oxygen. Thus, blood agents are poisons that effectively cause the body to suffocate. Examples of blood agents include: hydrogen cyanide (AC), cyanogens chloride (CK) and arsine (SA).

Nerve agents tend to block impulses between nerve cells or across synapses. They act primarily via absorption through the skin and lungs. Nerve agents are divided into two main groups: G-series agents and V-series agents so called due to their military designations. Nerve agents are the product of the search for improved chemical agents between the two World Wars. In the late 1930s German chemists synthesised the first nerve agents, tabun (GA) and sarin (GB), which were the first of the G-series agents. Soman (GD) and cyclosarin (GE and GF) followed quickly thereafter. British chemists developed V-series agents, which tend to be more lethal, in the 1950s. The series includes: VE, VG, VM and VX, which is the best-known agent. Some G-agents, particularly tabun and sarin, persist for only short periods. Other agents, such as soman and cyclosarin, persist longer and present a greater threat to the skin. V-agents, in comparison, are extremely potent (only milligrams needed to cause death) and persist for long periods of time on the battlefield as, in military parlance, “slime”.

CW agent group	Persistency	Rate of action
Choking agents:		
· (Cl) Chlorine	· Low	· Variable
· (PG) Phosgene	· Low	· Delayed
· (DP) Diphosgene	· Low	· Delayed
· (PS) Chloropicrin	· Low	· Rapid
Blister agents:		
· Sulphur mustard (H, HD)	· High Very	· Delayed
· Nitrogen mustard (HN)	· High	· Delayed
· Phosgene oxide (CX)	· Low	· Immediate
· Lewisite (L)	· High	· Rapid
Blood agents:		
· Hydrogen cyanide (AC)	· Low	· Rapid
· Cyanogen chloride (CK)	· Low	· Rapid
· Arsine (SA)	· Low	· Delayed
Nerve Agents		
· Tabun (GA)	· High	· Very rapid
· Sarin (GB)	· Low	· Very rapid
· Soman (GD)	· Moderate	· Very rapid
· Cyclosarin (GE, GF)	· Moderate	· Very rapid
· VX	· Very high	· Rapid

Radiological weapons

Radiological weapons spread radioactive material with the intent to kill or for disruptive purposes. In contrast to nuclear weapons which use a nuclear reaction to produce a large amount of energy and disburses radiological "daughter products", radiological weapons spread material that is already radioactive. The type of radiological weapons most commonly discussed is the so-called "dirty bomb" which uses conventional explosives to disperse radiological material. Considered useless for a state-sponsored army, these weapons are commonly referred to in the context of potential terrorist uses.

Modern proliferation threats and export control responses

WMD proliferation refers to the spread of nuclear, biological, chemical and radiological weapons. The threat of WMD proliferation has dramatically transformed since the end of the Cold War, especially as regards a nuclear threat. While the power dynamics between the two former superpowers, the United States and the USSR, was centred on the concept of mutually-assured destruction (MAD) whereby nuclear war could be averted by the promise of forceful reprisal in case of attack, the new post-Cold War era is marked by a set of more threatening issues that makes the need for strong nuclear export controls all the more necessary.

Even if the "official" nuclear-weapons States work towards disarmament in terms of the sheer quantity of their weapons, nuclear proliferation increases the risk of a nuclear explosion by spreading weapons across boundaries to actors that may have a lower usage threshold or less stringent security and safeguards standards. When broken down into specific threats, proliferation increases the risk of a nuclear explosion by increasing the probability of the theft of nuclear material by terrorists or underground actors due to poorly guarded facilities, the encouragement of regional arms races, accidental launch, contamination, the sale of technology and equipment to other parties, or most obviously, the intentional instigation of nuclear war.[10]

There are no simple solutions to the problem of nuclear weapons proliferation, for example. Varying strategies exist, but none of them taken independently constitute an omnipotent solution that can rid the world of the risk that nuclear weapons pose. This results from precisely the fact that there are multiple reasons behind why States as well as non-state actors seek nuclear explosive devices in the post-Cold War era. Perhaps the best theoretical perspective on understanding reasons behind proliferation comes from Peter Lavoy, who believes that States are more likely to pursue nuclear weapons when national elites prove that nuclear weapons are: (a) feasible, (b) the best solution for increasing their country's global standing, (c) in harmony with their country's cultural and political priorities.[11] Non-state actors seek to acquire nuclear explosive devices for the obvious symbolic and material damage they can inflict on their purported enemies.

WMD export controls comprise a preventive, non-military, supply-side non-proliferation instrument. They are preventive because they seek to keep actors from acquiring the necessary material for WMD proliferation ends rather than trying to target the reason for which such an actor desires to proliferate, or by focusing on trying to convince, or force them, to relinquish whatever WMD militarisation programme they have. That said, export controls cannot achieve a preventive effect unilaterally, or even together with other non-proliferation instruments. If an actor had enough money, willpower, and other necessary resources, it might succeed in eventually acquiring WMD. With this in mind, export controls ideally delay the successful acquisition of the materials, equipment and technology necessary for WMD until circumstances change, and buy time for other non-proliferation strategies to bring results.

---

10 Ikle, F. C., "Second coming of the nuclear age", *Foreign Affairs* (75:1), 1996, p. 119-128.

11 Lavoy, P., "Nuclear proliferation over the next decade", *The Non-proliferation Review* (13:3), 2006, p. 433-454.

What is a dual-use item?

The term "dual-use" as applied to WMD export controls is often defined in different ways depending on the context. The term became widely used following the end of the Cold War, when the international community came face-to-face with new proliferation threats that required new ways of conceptualising export controls in practice. This section will give a brief background to the term and clarify its use as applied to WMD export controls.

A distinction must be made between dual-use as applied to WMD export controls as a whole and dual-use as applied to describing the dual nature of nuclear energy. For WMD and conventional weapons export control systems the term refers to items that have *both peaceful application and military application*. Even if these items have primary commercial or civil applications, they also have the potential for military or weapons applications. Certain milling and turning machines commonly used by manufacturing industries could be diverted to contribute to the elaboration of a WMD. Therefore, for countering such risks of diversion, the national authorities have to control and verify the declared end-use before granting an export authorisation. The lists of controlled items adopted by the Australia Group in 1988 or by the MTCR in 1987 were both based on this distinction even if, formally, the term "dual-use" was not employed. Other export control regimes followed and proceeded to the review of their list of controlled items. The term "dual-use items" appears more frequently but in its first meaning, which implies peaceful and non-peaceful uses. Nevertheless, the Wassenaar Arrangement, using it for the first time in 1995 for naming its list of controlled goods and technologies, still remains the only regime to refer expressly to the term, even if broadly used by national authorities and academia.

The nuclear energy itself has two uses: unlike other forms of energy, nuclear energy can be used for power generation as well as other civilian uses but can also be used for a nuclear weapon. While nuclear energy does have a dual-use nature, this is distinct from the way that dual-use is discussed in reference to WMD export controls.

Dual-use export controls were defined as such mostly due to events that took place during the Gulf War in Iraq in 1991. After the war, the international community realised that it had failed to prevent Iraq from skirting existing export control guidelines in order to build a clandestine nuclear weapons program. At the time, export controls affected mostly "trigger list" items, that is, items directly used for WMD that would "trigger" export controls.

The international community's revelation of the Iraqi nuclear program spurred a different way of thinking about the role of export controls. Iraq's territory contains a generous supply of natural uranium compounds and its infrastructure allowed for the construction of industrial-scale facilities necessary for a nuclear weapons programme. In addition, its highly educated workforce provided the domestic research and development capability needed for such a complex undertaking. These indigenous capabilities allowed Iraq to evade the suspicion of the international community by producing most of the single-use military items integral to its nuclear weapons programme.[12] However, Iraq needed to import many items that at the time were not controlled by the international community, many of which were not conspicuously required for a nuclear weapons programme and therefore did not lead to suspicion. For example, Iraq succeeded in domestically constructing a uranium enrichment facility that used the process of electromagnetic isotope separation (EMIS).[13] In order to not have to deal with export control regimes like the Nuclear Suppliers Group or raise eyebrows concerning its activities, Iraq imported iron-pole magnets for use in EMIS, which it then adapted to final specifications domestically.

Following the Gulf War and the discovery of how Iraq was able to develop an indigenous nuclear weapons programme by taking advantage of uncontrolled trade, the Nuclear Suppliers Group, with the help of the IAEA, began identifying a list of non-nuclear items with legitimate civilian applications that could also be used in a WMD programme, or, in the NSG context, dual-use items. These items were incorporated into INFCIRC/254 Part 2 of the NSG control list, although an explicit definition of dual-use does not exist in the document. On the official website of the NSG, the description of dual-use is "items that can make a major contribution to an unsafeguarded nuclear fuel cycle or nuclear explosive activity, but which have non-nuclear uses as well, for example in industry".[14]

The European Union further institutionalised the term "dual-use", using it in the title of the EU Regulation 428/2009. In the Regulation, dual-use is defined as "items, including software and technology, which can be used for both civil and military purposes. This term also includes all goods which can be used for both non-explosive uses and assisting in any way in the manufacture of nuclear weapons or other nuclear explosive devices".

---

12 Michel, Q., "The evolution of nuclear export control regimes: from export control list to catch-all clause", *Atoms for Peace: An International Journal*, 1.1, 2005, p. 74-83.

13 "Iraqi nuclear weapons". Federation of American Scientists. 3 November 1998. Available: http://www.fas.org/nuke/guide/iraq/nuclear/program.htm.

14 Source: http://www.nuclearsuppliersgroup.org/Leng/02-guide.htm.

The Legal Context

The World Trade Organisation principles and the export controls

Since the beginning of the 1950s, international trade agreements have always tended to reduce trade restrictions unilaterally established by States in order to control the flow of goods coming, leaving or passing through their territory. Various negotiations and agreements concluded since the first General Agreement on Tariffs and Trade Round (GATT) until the present Doha Agenda have more or less succeeded in substituting a set of international trade rules to national restrictions.

If for common goods and services – textiles, air transports, telecommunication – lifting trade barriers appeared necessary to establish an international trading system, it was nevertheless reckoned that some goods and services – weapons, dual-use items, diamonds, and cultural goods – could not be considered as regular goods. Therefore, for political reasons they had to be submitted or maintained under national limitations.

As a result, a general exception and a security exception have been introduced in the GATT allowing Contracting States to maintain or to adopt national restrictive measures.[1]

These exceptions are established by Article XX (general exception) and Article XXI (security exception) which are divided according to the item or the pursued political objective. Regarding trade of dual-use items, it is essentially the security exception that States or group of States use for adopting derogating measures.

Established by Article XXI, the security exception allows Contracting Parties to unilaterally derogate to GATT principles in certain circumstances.

The commitments to the United Nations sanctions

The first exception concerns the implementation of Contracting Parties' commitments under the United Nations (UN) Charter for the maintenance of peace and security. It essentially *implements Article 49*

1 Similar worded exception is contained in articles XIV and XIV bis of the General Agreement on Tariffs and Services (GATS).

of the UN Charter that enables the Security Council to decide what measures, excepting the use of armed forces, are to be employed to give effect to its decisions. They may *inter alia* include complete or partial interruption of economic relations. Such decisions might involve a ban on exports of weapons and related dual-use items, equipment for internal repression, a ban on provision of certain services, an import ban on diamonds, a set of restrictions on admission, freezing of funds and economic resources of certain persons. However, an export prohibition aspiring to constrain States either to withdraw sensitive decisions, or to adopt acts or to align policies which cause or could cause a breach of peace and security might appear in contradiction with GATT principles. Therefore, the Agreement contains a dedicated provision, which enables to adopt trade restrictions by Contracting Parties. National implementation of this provision is usually mentioned by Contracting Parties in their licencing notification documents, wherein they describe rules and procedures which impose import or export prohibition of goods coming from or going to certain countries. Indeed,

> Brazil's 1994 notification on import licencing notes that the import licencing system of Brazil applies for good entering from exported to any country except those covered by UN Embargoes. The import licencing notification of Cyprus similarly notes that imports from certain countries are prohibited in accordance with United Nations resolutions.[2]

The response to conflicting situations

The second exception established by Article XXI (b) iii concerns actions taken by Contracting Parties in *time of war or other emergency in international relations*. The use of this exception has been mentioned on several occasions. First by the 1970 Working Party Report on "Accession of the United Arab Republic" where it was raised in response to the Arab League's boycott against Israel, including industries trading therewith. The Report alleged that:

> The history of the Arab boycott was beyond doubt related to the extraordinary circumstances to which the Middle East area had been exposed. The state of war which had long prevailed in that area necessitated the resorting to this system/ [...] In view of the political character of this issue, the United Arab Republic did not wish to discuss it within GATT. [...] It would not be reasonable to ask that the United Arab Republic should

2 GATT Analytical Index: "Guide to Law and Practice", p. 605. Source: http://www.wto.org/english/res_e/booksp_e/gatt_ai_e/gatt_ai_e.htm.

do business with a firm that transferred all or part of its profits from sales to the United Arab Republic to an enemy country".[3]

Later in 1982, during the Falkland War between United Kingdom and Argentina, the European Economic Community and its Member States have indefinitely suspended Argentine imports into their territory. In the notification of their decision, they stated that: "(a) they have taken certain measures in the light of the situation addressed in the Security Council Resolution 502; (b) they have taken these measures on the basis of their inherent rights of which Article XXI of the General Agreement is a reflection".[4]

The Article XXI (b) iii has also been used in the conflict between Nicaragua and the United States in May 1985 when the US adopted an executive order prohibiting all imports of goods and services of Nicaraguan origin, all exports from the US to or destined for Nicaragua and transactions relating thereto. Finally in 1991, the European Community notified restrictive trade measures and economic sanctions against Yugoslavia based on Article XXI (b) iii, considering that the war situation prevailing in the country no longer permits the preferential treatment to be upheld. Similar decisions were also taken by Australia, Austria, Canada, Finland, Japan, New Zealand, Norway, Sweden and the United States.

Most of the cases of Article XXI (b) iii implementation were related to internal repression or military conflict. However, it does not necessary mean that it concerns actions exclusively for the prevention or suppression of certain conflicts. An example of other potential action was referred to in a document published in 2004 concerning the TRIPS[5] agreement which embraces Article 73 holding a similar provision to that of GATT.

> The debate on IPRs and access to essential medicines, pandemics such as HIV may pose fundamental threats to the very existence of vulnerable societies. In such cases, it might be possible to invoke the Article 73 security exception for the protection of a nation's essential security interests. Arguably, pandemics such as HIV could be qualified as 'emergencies in international relations' as provided under Article 73(b)(iii) (the international

---

3 Working Party Report L/3362, adopted on 27 February 1970, 17S/33, 39, Paragraph 22 quoted by GATT Analytical Index: "Guide to Law and Practice", p. 603.

4 Communication to the Members of the GATT Council (18 May 1982 - L/5319/Rev.1). Available: http://www.wto.org/gatt_docs/English/SULPDF/90990462.pdf.

5 Trade-Related Aspects of Intellectual Property Right.

relations component being the failure to obtain adequate supplies of medicines within the framework of the multilateral institutional structure).[6]

Another potential action undertaken by a Contracting Parties with reference to *other emergency in international relations* might be illustrated by the adoption in 1996 of the US Cuban Liberty and Democratic Solidarity Act ("Helms-Burton Act"). Even, if the World Trade Organisation's (WTO) dispute settlement mechanisms did take the issue, the United States have mentioned the possibility to use Article XXI (b) iii if the European Union had brought the Helms-Burton Act before a WTO panel. The main purpose of this Act, as stated by Section 3 thereof is, in particular, "to assist the Cuban people in regaining their freedom and prosperity, as well as in joining the community of democratic countries that are flourishing in the Western Hemisphere". It should be noticed, that the core of the dispute was not an incompatibility with the exception established by Article XXI of a possibility to take actions constraining a third State to change its political regime. Actually, the main issue was another provision of this act which aimed at preventing foreign businesses and in particular EU industries from engaging in Cuban trade ventures involving property or assets expropriated by Fidel Castro's Government in the years following his takeover.

The fissionable materials

The third and the fourth exceptions established by Article XXI touch upon the sensitive nature of certain categories of goods. Indeed, the third exception concerns *fissionable materials or materials from which they are derived*, which might appear surprising as long as it is the only energy source to benefit from the GATT security exception. Most probably, this provision might be explained by historical reasons. In 1947 when the agreement was negotiated, only two years had passed since the first atomic explosion. Therefore, fissile materials were chiefly deemed to have military applications. Moreover, it was thought that the quantity thereof available worldwide might be rather limited and essentially concentrated in few countries (*i.e.* Canada, Congo and Australia). Thus, even if their use as a source of electricity production was acknowledged, fissile materials appeared to negotiators as strategic rather than peaceful use items. That is the reason why they were assimilated to a potential implement of war which should benefit from GATT derogations.

---

6 Document published by iprsonline.org, author unknown. Available: http://www.iprsonline.org/unctadictsd/docs/6.6Securityexpectations_update.pdf.

The traffic in arms, ammunition and implements of war

The fourth exception involves the *traffic in arms, ammunition and implements of war and to such traffic in others goods and materials as is carried on directly or indirectly for the purpose of supplying a military establishment.* The exact meaning of terms "arms" and "implements of war" was also controversial among Contracting Parties. The concept of "implement of war" was specifically applied by the United States in 1949 for imposing an embargo on export of strategic goods to Czechoslovakia. The strategic list including more than 200 entries appeared for Czechoslovak authorities so extensive that it was impossible to define which categories of items it covered exactly.[7] Nevertheless,

> [in] the discussion the Chairman indicated that Article XXI "embodied exception to the general rule contained in Article I". It was stated, inter alia, that "every country must be the judge in the last resort on questions relating to its own security" (CP.3/SR.22, p. 7). The claim that the United States had failed to carry out its obligations under the General Agreement through its administration of the issuance of export licences, was rejected by roll-call vote (17 to 1, with 3 abstentions) (CP.3/SR.22, p. 9).[8]

The extensive approach of the list of items that could fall under this exception seems to have been the one chosen by the negotiators, provided that during the discussion a question was raised

> whether the phrase 'for the purpose of supplying a military establishment' would permit restrictions on the export of iron ore when it was believed that the ore would be used by ordinary smelting works and ultimately for military purposes by another country. It was stated in response that 'if a Member exporting commodities is satisfied that the purpose of the transaction has to supply a military establishment, immediately or ultimately, this language would cover it.[9]

Most of Contracting Parties have adopted restrictive rules dedicated to the export of strategic goods that include a lengthy list of items to control. Such lists contained, on the one hand, items being undoubtedly implements of war, like machine guns or fighting aircrafts. On the other hand, it included items which could eventually contribute to the development, production of implements of war, like certain lasers, digital computers or telecommunication systems.

---

7 See Alexandroff, A. S., Sharma, R., *The World Trade Organization: Legal, Economic and Political Analysis*, Springer US, 2005, p. 1574.

8 Article XXI note by the Secretariat, 18 August 1987 (MTN.GNG/NG7/W/16).

9 GATT Analytical Index: "Guide to Law and Practice", p. 603.

These lists were usually the national implementation of strategic goods lists adopted within informal agreements gathering States attempting to coordinate their export control policies against States non-party to the concerned agreement. Initially, the control of certain strategic goods was suggested by the United States to NATO members to counter the risk that the US technology could be transferred directly or indirectly to a Warsaw Pact Member or to another sensitive country, such as China. This system called "Coordinating Committee for Multilateral Export Controls" (COCOM) was created in 1950. The main principle thereof was to ban the export of sensitive items, mostly military related, to the Soviet Union and its allies. Similar mechanisms dedicated to the fight against the proliferation of weapons of mass destruction have been adopted since then and their impact on international trade has never decreased.

The protection of essential security interests

Finally, the fifth exception that Contracting Party may invoke in order to derogate to GATT principles concerns any action, including the *disclosure of any information, that it considers necessary for the protection of its essential security interests.* This exception was implemented by the United States in its conflict with Czechoslovakia about the US restriction on export of strategic goods to certain countries. The US representative stated that "Article XXI [...] provides that a contracting party shall not be required to give information which it considers contrary to its security interest – and to the security interest of other ally countries – to reveal the names of the commodities that it considers to be most strategic".[10] The field of implementation of this exception is not restricted to certain categories of items and appears to be relevant for any action that the authorities might consider necessary for the protection of national security.

The definition of items concerned by the exceptions of Article XXI does not seem to be controversial. The interpretation of the notion of "essential security interest", which conditions the resort to Article XXI (a) (information) and (b) (fissile material, implement of war and emergency) upon the adoption of national restrictive measures, has been discussed more than once. However, Contracting Parties have never succeeded in adopting a common understanding of this term. In 1961, Ghana adopted a ban on import of Portuguese goods which was motivated "under the provisions of Article XXI (b) (iii), noting that 'under this Article each contracting party was the sole judge of what was necessary in its essential security interests' (SR.19/12, page 196).

[10] Quoted by the GATT Analytical Index: "Guide to Law and Practice", p. 602.

The statement by Ghana on the invocation of Article XXI was noted by the Contracting Parties".[11] Similar embargo and boycott decisions adopted by Egypt against Israel (1970), by European Communities' Member States, Australia and Canada against Argentina (1982), by the United States against Cuba (1962) and Nicaragua (1985), were motivated by the defence of "essential security interest". The reason might ensue from the jurisdictional argument so far unresolved, "relied more than once by the United States – that the phrase 'it considers necessary' in the chapeau of paragraph (b) means that a country's decision to take action on national security ground under XXI (b) cannot be challenged in the dispute resolution system".[12]

As concerns the conformity of measures adopted by States with the spirit of Article XXI, the sole issue was discussed when Sweden introduced in 1975 a global import quota system for certain footwear.

> The Swedish Government considered that the measure was taken in conformity with the spirit of Article XXI and stated, *inter alia*, that the "decrease in domestic production has become a threat to the planning of Sweden's economic defence in situations of emergency as an integral part of its security policy. This policy required the maintenance of a minimum domestic production capacity in vital industries" (L/4250). In the Council "many representatives expressed doubts as to the justification of these measures under the General Agreement" (C/M/109).[13]

Hence States appear to be rather free to define what might fall under their national security interests.

The United Nations interventions for peace and security

Export control of weapons and dual-use items have been considered formally by the United Nations Security Council at the end of the 1980s essentially within the framework of embargo resolutions. Initially, the Security Council was not referring to the term weapons but invited in certain resolutions States to "restraint and to refrain from any act which may lead to a further escalation and widening of the conflict".[14] It was not before the use of chemical weapons in the conflict between Iraq and Islamic Republic of Iran that the Security Council adopted a resolution calling "upon all States to continue to apply or to establish strict control of the export to the parties to the conflict strict controls of chemical

---

11 Article XXI, note by the Secretariat, 18 August 1987 (MTN.GNG/NG7/W/16), p. 5.

12 Alexandroff, A. S., Sharma, R., *op. cit.*, p. 1575.

13 Article XXI, note by the Secretariat, 18 August 1987 (MTN.GNG/NG7/W/16), p. 6.

14 See Paragraph 4 of United Nations Security Council Resolution (UNSCR) 479 of 28 September 1980.

products serving for the production of chemicals weapons".[15] This Resolution was followed in 1991 by two fundamental decisions of the Security Council that initiated the regular adoption of formal arms and WMD-related items' embargo resolutions. The first was related to the situation in Yugoslavia for which it was decided under Chapter VII of the Charter that all States shall "immediately implement a general and complete embargo on all deliveries of weapons and military equipment".[16] The second one, also based on Chapter VII, concerned Kuwait's restoration of sovereignty and strengthening measures against Iraq. It contains detailed provisions on the dismantle of the Iraqi WMD research programme but also strengthened embargo measures by adding items and technology useful for the development of chemical, biological and nuclear weapons as well as their means of delivery.[17]

Since then, the Security Council has regularly adopted constraining embargoes on arms and related items[18] or on WMD dual-use items.[19]

The Security Council's ability to take decisions set in Article 24 of the UN Charter suggests that its competencies are not limited to those foreseen in Chapter VII, but extend to all measures considered necessary to maintain or restore peace.[20] Apart from a few exceptions, such as the UNSC Resolution 1540, the Security Council rather has a case-by-case approach.[21] The Security Council can enact resolutions, which are considered as sources of international law and are directly binding.[22] In general the mandatory measures contained in the resolutions are subject to regular review and can even expire.

The United Nations Security Council Resolution 1540 (2004)

On 28 April 2004, the United Nations Security Council adopted Resolution 1540 under the Chapter VII of the UN Charter, for a period

---

15 UNSCR 612 of 9 May 1988.

16 UNSCR 713 of 25 September 1991.

17 See paragraph 24 of the UNSCR 687 of 3 April 1991.

18 See for example: UNSCR 788 of 19 November 1992 (Liberia), UNSCR 918 (Rwanda) of 17 May 1994, UNSCR 1572 of 15 November 2005 (Ivory Coast).

19 See for example: UNSCR 1718 of 14 October 2006 (Democratic People's Republic of Korea), UNSCR 1737 of 23 December 2006.

20 Daillier, P., Pellet, A., *Droit International Public*, Paris, L.G.D.J., 5th edition, 1994, p. 366.

21 Zimmermann, A., Elberling, B., "Grenzen der Legislativbefugnisse des Sicherheitsrates: Resolution 1540 und abstrakte Bedrohungen des Weltfriedens", *Vereinte Nationen* 3/2004, p. 74.

22 Daillier, P., Pellet, A., *op. cit.*, p. 360 and following.

of two years.[23] This resolution aims mainly at preventing non-state actors from acquiring unconventional weapons, related materials and means of delivery. The Council also decided that all States would have to establish domestic controls to prevent proliferation of WMD and their means of delivery, in particular for terrorist purposes. This includes the establishment of appropriate controls over related materials. To this end, all UN Member States are required to adopt legislative as well as other binding or non-binding measures of domestic control to fulfil their obligations in relation to arms control and disarmament, to prevent proliferation in all aspects of WMD and to implement enforcement measures.

> It also encourages enhanced international cooperation on such efforts. The resolution affirms support for the multilateral treaties whose aim is to eliminate or prevent the proliferation of WMD and the importance for all States to implement them fully; it reiterates that none of the obligations in resolution 1540 (2004) shall conflict with or alter the rights and obligations of State Parties to the Treaty on the Non-Proliferation of Nuclear Weapons, the Chemical Weapons Convention, or the Biological Weapons Convention or alter the responsibilities of the IAEA and OPCW.[24]

The UN Secretary General Kofi Annan described the Resolution 1540 together with the Proliferation Security Initiative simply as a welcomed supplementary effort to the realisation of the goals of the Non-Proliferation Treaty. In the report "In Larger Freedom: Towards Development, Security and Human Rights for All" to the UN General Assembly in March 2005 he stated that "while the Treaty on the Non-Proliferation of Nuclear Weapons remains the foundation of the non-proliferation regime, we should welcome recent efforts to supplement it. These include Security Council resolution 1540 (2004)".[25]

For others, this resolution represents the most far-reaching international policy re-orientation since the Non-proliferation Treaty of Nuclear Weapons.[26] Even if it does not define conditions of supply or list of items to control, some of its provisions could be considered as the framework for a model of export control regime to be implemented by States.

---

[23] Security Council Resolution S/RES/1540 (2004), Paragraph 4.

[24] Source: http://www.un.org/en/sc/1540/index.shtml.

[25] Report of the UN Secretary-General on 21 March 2005, "In larger freedom: towards development, security and human rights for all", A/59/2005, paragraph 100.

[26] Olberg, L., "Implementing Resolution 1540: What the National Reports Indicate", Disarmament Diplomacy, Issue 82, Spring 2006 with reference to Miller, A., Morten Bremer, M., "Nuclear Non-Proliferation and United Nations Security Council Resolution 1540", in "NUPI Policy Briefs on the Implementation of the Treaty of the Non-Proliferation of Nuclear Weapons", April 2005, p. 35.

The 1540 Committee

In accordance with operative Paragraph 4 of the Resolution,

> [...] For a period of no longer than two years, a Committee of the Security Council, consisting of all members of the Council, which will, calling as appropriate on other expertise, report to the Security Council for its examination, on the implementation of this resolution, and to this end calls upon States to present a first report no later than six months from the adoption of this resolution to the Committee on steps they have taken or intend to take to implement this resolution.

The Security Council extended the mandate of the so-called "1540 Committee"[27] for ten years by unanimously adopting Resolution 1977 (2011). Before that, the mandate of the 1540 Committee had already been extended twice – for two and three additional years – by Resolution 1673 (2006) and Resolution 1810 (2008). In the Resolution 1540, the Security Council also requested the Committee to "consider a comprehensive review of the status of implementation of (the) Resolution".[28] As a result of this process, a final document was published on the 1540 Committee website. Through Resolution 1810 (2008), the Security Council "urged the 1540 Committee to continue strengthening its role in facilitating technical assistance, including by engaging actively in matching offers and requests for assistance, therefore strengthening its clearinghouse function".[29] The full implementation of resolution 1540 (2004) by all States is a long-term process that will require continuous efforts at national, regional and international levels. Therefore, Resolution 1977 (2011) organises the planning of two comprehensive reviews, one after five years and one before the end of the mandate. Additionally, the 1540 Committee is mandated by resolution 1977 (2011) to "continue to strengthen its role to facilitate the provision of technical assistance and to enhance cooperation with relevant international organisations" as well as continuing "to refine its outreach efforts, and to continue to institute transparency measures".[30]

Other international legal instruments

International export control regimes of sensitive items are ruled by three international treaties dedicated respectively to nuclear, chemical and biological weapons. These treaties essentially set principles to be

---

27 Ambassador and Permanent Representative of the Republic of Korea to the United Nations, Kim Sook, chairs the Committee as of April 2013.

28 1540 Committee, Main page, http://www.un.org/en/sc/1540/index.shtml.

29 *Idem.*

30 *Idem.*

implemented individually by States signatories. To avoid the risk of inconsistency between national regimes when implementing their treaties commitments, several soft law instruments have been established by potential suppliers States of those items. The analysis of the soft law instruments can be found in the next chapter.

The Non-Proliferation Treaty (NPT)

The cornerstone of the internationally binding set of agreements in the nuclear sector is the Non-Proliferation Treaty (NPT). The Treaty pursues three fundamental aims:

- Preventing the spread of nuclear weapons and weapons technology through the ban of acquisition and controls;
- Disarmament of the existing nuclear military capacities;
- The vested right of peaceful uses of nuclear energy by the Member States of the NPT.

Adopted on 12 June 1968 in New York, the NPT came into force in March 1970. It has been signed and ratified by 190 States. India, Israel, North Korea and Pakistan have declined to ratify since they are not ready to dismantle their – alleged – nuclear weapons programmes. Only States that had manufactured and exploded a nuclear weapon or other nuclear explosive devices prior to 1st January 1967 could be considered under the words of the Treaty as having the right to detain nuclear weapons.[31] The Treaty has never been amended since its adoption, and every five years a review conference of State Parties is convened in order to analyse the different provisions of the Treaty and define the political actions to be undertaken for its effective and universal implementation. A final document is usually adopted by consensus and brings new light to the understanding of certain Treaty provisions.

Each non nuclear-weapon State Party to the Treaty has to accept safeguards as set forth in an agreement to be negotiated and concluded with the International Atomic Energy Agency (IAEA). The objectives of the safeguards are to verify, through reporting, on-site verifications and accounting systems that fissile materials are not diverted to prohibited use under the NPT.

With regard to the experience gained after the Iraqi case in the 1990s, the safeguards system revealed its weaknesses. Therefore, the IAEA developed a model of Additional Protocol to the bilateral safeguards agreement that gives the possibility to the IAEA, through supplementary negotiated information obligations and control measures, to more easily reach conclusions on possibly undeclared activities

---

[31] Treaty of Non-Proliferation of Nuclear Weapons, Article IX.3.

undertaken in the nuclear sector or concerning undeclared nuclear material of a State Party. The State Parties are called upon to report extensively about all aspects concerning their nuclear activities and activities in the framework of the nuclear fuel cycle.[3233]

In its Article III.2 the NPT includes two commitments to be implemented by the State Parties. The first one is an obligation to control the transfers toward non nuclear-weapon States as understood by the Treaty of "source or special fissionable material, and equipment or material especially designed or prepared for the processing, use or production of special fissionable material". The Treaty did not provide a definition of what shall be encompassed by these two categories of items. Nevertheless, a statement has been adopted at the end of the 2010 NPT Review Conference, which establishes that the list of controlled items does not include nuclear-related dual-use items, even if such items "are relevant to the proliferation of nuclear weapons and therefore to the Treaty as a whole. The Conference calls upon all States' parties to ensure that their exports of nuclear-related dual-use items to States not party to the Treaty do not assist any nuclear weapons programmes".[34]

The second commitment undertaken by the States consists of the obligation to condition the export of nuclear items to the submission of fissile materials, being used in the facilities where the items are to be transferred, to safeguards. A Comprehensive Safeguards Agreement has been considered, at the NPT 2000 Review Conference, as the set of safeguards required by the words of the Treaty: "transfer of source or special fissionable material or equipment or material [...] to non-nuclear-weapon States should require, as a necessary precondition, acceptance of the comprehensive IAEA safeguards". The Additional Protocol is not yet considered as a condition of supply even if the "Conference notes that many States recognise that comprehensive safeguards agreements and additional protocols are among the integral elements of the IAEA safeguards system".[35]

---

32 Source: http://www.un.org/en/conf/npt/2005/npttreaty.html; http://www.iaea.org/Publications/Documents/Treaties/npt.html.

33 Up to April 2013, 140 States (plus Taiwan) signed the Additional Protocol. It is in force in 109 States (plus Taiwan), including all EU Member States. Source: http://www.auswaertiges-amt.de/sid_6597F4F5B425897E8F874E1EE52434C7/DE/Aussenpolitik/Friedenspolitik/Abruestung/Nukleares/IAEO_node.html#doc349416bodyText3; http://www.world-nuclear.org/info/inf12.html.

34 2010 Review Conference of the Parties to the Treaty on the Non-Proliferation of Nuclear Weapons, Final Document, Vol. 1, New York, 2010.

35 *Idem.*

The Biological Weapons Convention (BWC)

International efforts to constrain the proliferation of biological weapons is closely linked to the challenge of the chemical weapons non-proliferation. Indeed, the Protocol for the Prohibition of the Use in War of Asphyxiating, Poisonous or Other Gases, and of Bacteriological Methods of Warfare, signed in Geneva on 17 June 1925, was also dedicated to biological weapons. It condemned explicitly: "the use in war of asphyxiating, poisonous or other gases, and of all analogous liquids materials or devices".

Export control regulations *per se* appeared in 1972[36] with the adoption of the Convention on the Prohibition of the Development, Production and stockpiling of Bacteriological and Toxin Weapons and their Destruction (BWC).[37] Article III of the Convention states explicitly that State Parties should not transfer "to any recipient whatsoever, directly or indirectly, and not in any way to assist, encourage, or induce any State, group of States or international organisations to manufacture or otherwise acquire any of agents, toxins, weapons, equipment or their means of delivery". By "biological weapons", it should be understood the necessary destruction material such as microbial or other biological agents or toxins whatever their origin or method of production of types and in quantities that have no justification for prophylactic, protective or other peaceful purposes. Are also included in the scope of the Convention the weapon equipment or means of delivery designed to use such agents or toxins for hostile purposes or in armed conflict.

Although the Convention does not contain any verification mechanism, State Parties must rely on intelligence assessments to determine whether or not others are complying with the Convention. Since the first review conference,[38] doubts and concerns have arisen in particular about the former Soviet Union, Iraq, North Korea, Libya and Syria. In 1994, an *ad hoc* group was established in order to design and conclude a legally binding protocol to strengthen the Convention. Negotiations were conducted for six and half years and ended up with the adoption of a set of monitoring and verifications mechanisms which, if it had been adopted, should help deterring countries from pursuing illegal biological programmes. Unfortunately, the project was globally rejected by the United States in September 2001.

---

[36] The Convention entered into force in 1975.

[37] As of April 2013, 171 countries had signed the BWC while 155 had ratified it. Source: http://www.opbw.org/.

[38] Review conferences of the Convention are convened every five years.

The Chemical Weapons Convention (CWC)

While the Convention on the Prohibition of the Development, Production, Stockpiling and Use of Chemical Weapons and on their Destruction (otherwise known as the Chemical Weapons Convention or CWC) entered into force only in 1997, its origins date back to the Geneva Protocol of 1925,[39] which was the first treaty prohibiting the use of chemical and biological weapons. The period between the World War II and the late 1960s was not used for improving and expanding the scope of the Geneva Protocol. Discussions and negotiations resumed only with the Geneva Conference on Disarmament in 1968 and continued until January 1993, when the CWC was opened for signature in Paris. In 1997, the first 87 State Parties enabled the CWC to enter into force.[40] In order to accompany the implementation, a permanent organisation was created: the Organisation for the Prohibition of Chemical Weapons (OPCW).

For the first time a multilateral convention succeeded not only to ban an entire category of WMD but to provide as well an international verification mechanism regarding the destruction of these weapons. Because of the involvement of the global chemical industry during the negotiation process of the CWC, the industry keeps on supporting and cooperating with the main instances within the CWC industrial verification regime. To this end, industrial facilities are inspected to ensure that toxic chemicals are used exclusively for peaceful purposes.[41]

Principles

The CWC is based on four principles. The first principle is the *prohibition of the development, production, acquisition, stockpiling, retention, transfer and use of chemical weapons*. This principle includes a commitment by each State Party not to undertake in the development, production, or transfer – directly or indirectly – of chemical weapons to anyone and not to assist, encourage or induce, in any way, anyone to engage in any activity prohibited to a State Party under the Convention.[42]

---

39 The Protocol for the Prohibition of the Use in War of Asphyxiating, Poisonous or other Gases, and of Bacteriological Methods of Warfare, usually called the Geneva Protocol; First treaty prohibiting the use of chemical and biological weapons.

40 Weith, N., Wegner, C., Ehrlich, W. (eds.), "Grundzüge der Exportkontrolle", Köln 2006, p. 38-39, 254-255. As of April 2013, 184 States are parties to the CWC. Source: http://www.opcw.org/news-publications/publications/history-of-the-chemical-weapons-convention/.

41 Source: http://www.opcw.org/news-publications/publications/history-of-the-chemical-weapons-convention/.

42 Preamble and articles I and V of the CWC.

The second principle is the obligation to *destroy chemical weapons and production facilities*, that State Parties own, possess or abandoned on the territory of another State Party.[43]

The third principle consists of the promotion of *free trade in chemicals as well as international cooperation and exchange of scientific and technical information* in the field of chemical activities for purposes not prohibited under the Convention, in order to stimulate the economic and technological development of all State Parties[44]

The fourth principle is the right acknowledged for each State Party to *develop, produce, otherwise acquire, retain, transfer and use toxic chemicals and their precursors* for purposes not prohibited under this Convention.[45] These authorised purposes could be of the following nature:

- *Peaceful*, such as in industrial, agricultural, research, medical, pharmaceutical applications;
- *Protective*, meaning directly related to the protection against toxic chemicals and against chemical weapons;
- *Military*, only if not connected with the use of chemical weapons and not dependent on the use of the toxic properties of chemicals as a method of warfare.

The CWC defined as *chemical weapons*, three categories of items – together or separately – which are:

- Toxic chemicals and their precursors, except where intended for purposes not prohibited under the Convention, as long as the types and quantities are consistent with such purposes. "Toxic chemical" means any chemical, which through its chemical action on life processes can cause death, temporary incapacity or permanent harm to humans or animals. This includes all such chemicals, regardless of their origin or of their method of production, and regardless of whether they are produced in facilities, in munitions or elsewhere. "Precursor" means any chemical reactant which takes part at any stage in the production by whatever method of a toxic chemical. This includes any key component of a binary or multicomponent chemical system. For the purpose of implementing the Convention toxic chemicals and precursors which have been identified for the application of verification measures are listed in the Annex on Chemicals of the CWC;

43 Preamble and articles IV and VI of the CWC.

44 Preamble and Article XI of the CWC.

45 Preamble and Article VI of the CWC.

- Munitions and devices specifically designed to cause death or other harm through the toxic properties of those toxic chemicals, which would be released as a result of the employment of such munitions and devices;
- Any equipment specifically designed for use directly in connection with the employment of munitions and toxic chemicals and their precursors.

The CWC also includes a definition of the "old chemical weapons"[46] and of the "abandoned chemical weapons"[47] for which simplified provisions are established.

The transfers of chemicals and safeguards

As it is the case for most non-proliferation instruments, the implementation of the commitments contained in the CWC lay under the sole responsibility of State Parties. The Convention precisely defines the measures that States have to adopt to encounter their obligations. Those measures deal in particular with:

- The prohibition of natural and legal persons anywhere on its territory or in any other place under its jurisdiction as recognised by international law from undertaking any activity prohibited to a State Party under the Convention, including enacting criminal legislation in connection to such activity;
- The prohibition of any activity prohibited to a State Party under the Convention in any place under State Party control;
- The extension of penal legislation to any activity prohibited to a State Party under this Convention undertaken anywhere by natural persons possessing its nationality in conformity with international law.

Regarding transfers of chemicals for lawful purposes, the Convention divided chemicals into three categories for which a specific regime is organised.

Category I[48] contains chemicals considered as very sensitive and for which State Parties shall not produce, acquire, retain or use them outside the territories of State-Parties and *shall not transfer such*

46 (a) Chemical weapons which were produced before 1925; or (b) Chemical weapons produced in the period between 1925 and 1946 that have deteriorated to such extent that they can no longer be used as chemical weapons.

47 Chemical weapons, including old chemical weapons, abandoned by a State after 1st January 1925 on the territory of another State without the consent of the latter.

48 See Annex on Chemicals (Schedule I) of the CWC. It listed eight groups of toxic chemicals such as sulfur mustards, lewisites, nitrogen mustards, saxitoxin, ricin and four groups of precursors such as chlorosarin and chlorosoman.

chemicals outside their territories except to another State Party.[49] Moreover, quantities of chemicals that State Parties could acquire is, be it through production or withdrawal from chemical weapons stocks and transfer, strictly limited to one ton per year. The production of such chemicals should be carried out at a single small-scale facility. The transfers of equipment specifically designed for use in connection with these chemicals is not submitted to specific conditions. Nevertheless, due to the general commitment not to assist, encourage or induce, in any way, anyone to engage in any activity forbidden by the Convention, it could be pretended that State Parties should not transfer such equipment, at least not to other State Parties.

Category II[50] contains chemicals considered so sensitive that State Parties have to *annually declare data on the quantities produced, processed, consumed, imported and exported of each chemicals listed*, as well as to provide a quantitative specification of import and export for each country involved. Similar to the first category, chemicals of category II should only be transferred to or received from State Parties. This obligation has taken effect in April 2001, three years after the entry into force of the Convention. Before that, it was possible to transfer to third States (not parties) as long as the supplier State ensured that the transferred chemicals could only be used for purposes not prohibited under the Convention and if the supplier required an end-use certificate from the recipient State.

Category III[51] contains chemicals considered as less sensitive, for which State Parties have, like Category II, *to annually declare data on quantities produced, imported and exported, as well as a quantitative specification of import and export for each country involved.* Transfers of Category III items to third States of the CWC are authorised if the suppliers ensure that the transferred chemicals can only be used for purposes not prohibited under this Convention. *Inter alia*, the supplier State shall require from the recipient State a certificate stating, in relation to the transferred chemicals:

---

64 See Part VI and the activities not prohibited under the Convention in accordance with Article VI.

50 See Annex on Chemicals (Schedule II) of the CWC. It lists three groups of toxic chemicals such as amiton, PFIB, BZ and eleven groups of precursors such as arsenic trichloride, thiodiglycol and pinacolyl alcohol.

51 See Annex on Chemicals (Schedule III) of the CWC. It lists toxic chemicals such as phosgene, carbonyl dichloride, cyanogen chloride, hydrogen cyanide, chloropicrin: trichloronitromethane and precursors: such as phosphorus oxychloride, phosphorus trichloride, phosphorus pentachloride, trimethyl phosphite, triethyl phosphite, dimethyl phosphite, diethyl phosphite, sulfur monochloride, sulfur dichloride, thionyl chloride, ethyldiethanolamine, methyldiethanolamine, triethanolamine.

- That they will only be used for purposes not prohibited under this Convention;
- That they will not be re-transferred;
- Their types and quantities;
- Their end-use(s); and
- The name(s) and address(es) of the end-user(s).

Since the CWC authorises State Parties to develop, produce, transfer and use toxic chemicals and their precursors for purposes not prohibited, a very specific verification system has been established. The system, which applies to all State Parties without exception is based on a series of obligations.

First, the State Parties must elaborate an initial declaration and annual declarations regarding the relevant chemicals and facilities. The content of these declarations is determined in function of the three categories of items.

Then, the State Parties must implement measures aiming at ensuring that the toxic chemicals and their precursors are only developed, produced, otherwise acquired, retained, transferred, or used for purposes not prohibited under this Convention. In this regard, each State Party has to designate or establish a national authority to serve as the national point of contact for effective liaison with the Organisation and the other State Parties.

Finally, a Technical Secretariat carries out the verification measures as provided in the Verification Annex of the CWC. These measures vary in function of the categories of toxic chemicals and their precursors listed, and may include systematic on-site inspections and monitoring with on-site instrument.[52]

The suspicion mechanism and sanctions

The CWC establishes in its Article IX a suspicion mechanism which authorises a State Party to request from the Executive Council[53] that it assists in clarifying any situation which may be considered ambiguous or which raises a concern about the possible non-compliance of another State Party with the Convention.[54] It should be pointed out that the

52 Article VIII D of the CWC.

53 The Convention, in its Article VIII establishes three bodies: the State Parties Conference, the Executive Council (which is composed of 41 delegates elected for two years by the Conference) and the Technical Secretariat.

54 Prior to any request to the Executive Council, States Parties are encouraged to solve among them any different on any matter which may raise such doubts about compliance with the Convention, or such concerns about a related matter which may be considered ambiguous.

CWC obligations are mostly negative – such as the obligation not to transfer items of Categories I and II to third States – and it appears rather unclear which "rights and privileges" the Convention could suspend, except the right to request and to receive assistance and protection against the use or threat of use of chemical weapons.[55]

Regarding sanctions against nationals which have undertaken prohibited activities, each State Party has to adopt the measures necessary to implement their obligations, including enacting penal legislation with respect to such prohibited activities.[56]

55 Article X of the CWC.

56 Article VII 1 of the CWC.

The International Export Control Fora

Conditions and Criteria

The export control regimes, structured in the form of *fora* of the most prominent supplying countries in the domain, aim at organising the constraints they seek to impose on them, with a view to conciliate the objective of a sound competition in trade and the non-proliferation of WMD.

One must note that these *fora* and the provisions they edict are often improperly referred to as stand-alone "regimes". However, and despite the names that can be given to these structures, the guidelines adopted cannot alone form a regime, which supposes that the set of rules would be directly applicable to the exporters. Formally, these guidelines can be considered, at the maximum, as "soft law" provisions. Substantially, the absence of prescriptive provisions regarding sanctions for the exporters found in breach of their obligations, for example, also prevent these guidelines from being directly applicable. Therefore, these international structures found trade control "systems" rather than proper "regimes". Despite the "soft" character of these instruments in the regulation of the international trade the constraints they impose on their export nevertheless constrain the freedom of importing of the third countries by a collateral effect.

In order to grant or not an authorisation, the States base their decisions on two types of considerations, which are the conditions and criteria designed by the international export control fora.

The conditions are *objective* elements that recipient countries have to meet in order to obtain an export authorisation from the supplier. These elements can be the ratification of a treaty, the conclusion of a safeguard agreement or the submission of an end-user certificate (EUC).

The criteria are *subjective* elements to be considered by the supplying State, through a case-by-case analysis, in order to authorise or not a transfer. The criteria can be the internal situation in the country of final destination, the existence of tensions or armed conflicts and the risk that the recipient country would use the proposed export aggressively against another country or to assert by force its territorial claim.

The origins and the Coordinating Committee for Multilateral Export Controls (COCOM)

The first export control regime set with the intention to restrict the trade toward another group of countries was the Coordinating Committee for Multilateral Export Controls (COCOM). It was founded under the impulse of the United States in 1949 in the context of the Cold War, without proper formal status. It was intended to prevent the export of high technology goods, such as nuclear industry items, conventional arms and dual-use goods, from NATO countries and their allies to countries of the Warsaw Pact. The end of the Cold War led to the dissolution of COCOM in 1994, replaced by the Wassenaar Arrangement, which focuses on more diffuse threats, meaning that it no longer deals with one single group of identified countries.[1]

Already during the Cold War, it was clear that the COCOM would not be sufficient to impede the acquisition of weapons of mass destructions by other countries. Therefore, the Zangger Committee, the Nuclear Suppliers Group, the Missile Technology Control Regime and the Australia Group have been founded and coordinate the implementation of the different international treaties and conventions dedicated to the non-proliferation of WMD.[2] These five international export control *fora* – which may be seen as "clubs" of commercially advanced countries – can be seen as the formal and substantial backbone of the trade control systems. All these instances, however, issue non-binding rules from a purely legal perspective. They seek consensus and the uniform application by the participating States of the guidelines thus adopted. The rules it issues are merely binding from a political perspective.[3]

Within the *fora*, the decisions reflect the consensus of the participating countries and, therefore, constitute control standards regarding the lists of goods to be controlled and the organisation of the licencing procedures. In these structures, moreover, the participants set procedures for the exchange of information and facilitate cooperation amongst them. For instance, the obligation to report on some decisions taken at the national level – *e.g.* denial of export authorisations – guarantees a certain transparency inside the regime.[4]

---

1 Weith, N., Wegner, C., Ehrlich, W. (eds.), "Grundzüge der Exportkontrolle", Köln, 2006, p. 48 and following.

2 *Idem.*

3 *Idem.*

4 *Idem.*

The Zangger Committee (ZC)

The Zangger Committee was founded between 1972 and 1974, following the entering into force of the nuclear Non-Proliferation Treaty, to serve as the "faithful interpreter" of its Article III.2 and, thus to harmonise the nuclear export control policies of the NPT Parties. It was named after its first Chairman, Professor Claude Zangger. It includes 38 participating countries,[5] including all the nuclear weapon States, and the European Commission is a permanent observer.

The Committee meets once a year in Vienna and discusses the ways to reach a common understanding on the two conditions of supply required by article III.2 of the NPT for conciliating non-proliferation goals and sound competition.

The first condition that is discussed relates to the definition of what constitutes "equipment or material especially designed or prepared for the processing, use or production of special fissionable material", as it was not comprehensively defined by the NPT. In this regard, the Committee has drafted a list of nuclear items and technology that shall be submitted for export authorisation in the participating countries. Since its adoption, this list has been review and updated regularly and constitutes presently standard requirements for NPT States parties.

The second condition relates to the category of safeguards in force that suppliers should require from a recipient State in order to authorise the export of listed items. The Committee considers that the Comprehensive Safeguards Agreement (CSA) should be the minimum safeguards level to be requested.

The Nuclear Suppliers Group (NSG)

The NSG, originally named as the *London Club*, was founded in 1975 in reaction to the explosion by India of a nuclear weapon in 1974. The context, then, was the fear that the number of States owning such weapons could increase without possible control in the future. The *fora*, which is a duplication somehow of the Zangger Committee, was created because France, which was already considered to be a major supplier of nuclear goods and technology at that time, had not signed the NPT and, consequently, was not taking part to the Zangger Committee either. The NSG was a way to persuade France to undertake the same commitments as its main competitors in the nuclear sphere.

The NSG has adopted two groups of guidelines. The first set of guidelines governs the export of items that are *especially designed or*

---

5 As of April 2013.

prepared for nuclear use (called the "trigger list").[6] The second set rules the export of *nuclear-related dual-use items and technologies*, which are items that are *normally destined for a non-nuclear use*. However, in certain circumstances, they can also make a major contribution to an unsafeguarded nuclear fuel cycle activity or nuclear explosive activity.[7]

The NSG guidelines impose an obligation to submit for a national export authorisation all exports of items listed in both trigger and dual-use lists. Whereas both guidelines do not include a formal prohibition, suppliers are invited to adopt a restrictive policy regarding transfers of sensitive items especially if actual denials have been issued by one or more NSG States. *Sensitive items* are defined rather broadly as items "usable for nuclear weapons or other nuclear explosive devices".

In principle, exports to States allegedly detaining nuclear weapons are prohibited except to the five States recognised as nuclear weapon States by the Nuclear Non-Proliferation Treaty (China, France, Russia, the United Kingdom and the United States of America). Since September 2008, an additional exception has been included in the NSG Guidelines authorising transfers of all items listed in the trigger and the dual-use lists to India.[8]

While deciding whether or not to authorise a transfer, supplier States should examine the licence application for trigger list items in the light of the *non-proliferation principle*, which invites suppliers to authorise a transfer only when they estimate that it would not contribute to the proliferation of nuclear weapons or other nuclear explosive devices or would not be diverted to an act of nuclear terrorism.

Suppliers should also refuse a transfer if there are potential *risks of retransfer* due to the failure of the recipient State to develop and maintain appropriate and effective national export and transhipment controls as identified by UNSCR 1540. Complementarily, the

> Suppliers should exercise a policy of restraint in the transfer of sensitive facilities, equipment, technology and material usable for nuclear weapons or other nuclear explosive devices, especially in cases when a State has on its

---

6 IAEA, INFCIRC/254/Rev.10/Part 1, Communications Received from Certain Member States Regarding Guidelines for the Export of Nuclear Material, Equipment and Technology.

7 IAEA, INFCIRC/254/Rev.8/Part 2, Communications Received from Certain Member States Regarding Guidelines for Transfers of Nuclear-Related Dual-Use Equipment, Materials, Software and Related Technology.

8 For more details, see document IAEA, INFCIRC/734 (corrected).

territory entities that are the object of active NSG Guidelines Part 2 denial notifications from more than one NSG Participating Government.[9]

Before granting an authorisation, a supplier State should verify if the recipient State fulfils the *export conditions* defined by the NSG guidelines. These conditions are different for trigger list items and dual-use items.

Conditions of supply for NSG trigger list items

The first condition of supply for trigger list items concerns the obligation for a recipient State to bring into force an agreement with the IAEA requiring the application of *safeguards* on all sources and special fissionable material in its current and future peaceful activities (Comprehensive Safeguards Agreement).

This condition contains one exception with regards to the transfers toward non nuclear-weapon States when they are "deemed essential for the safe operation of existing facilities and only if safeguards are applied to those facilities". Before granting such authorisation, suppliers should inform and, if appropriate, consult each other in case they intend to authorise or to deny such transfers. This exception, which is called the "grand-father clause", has been used twice by Russia to supply fissile material for a nuclear power plant to India in 2000 and 2006.

Even if the current adoption of safeguards based on the Additional Protocol does not constitute a NSG Guidelines' condition of supply for all trigger list items, it is presently required by all EU Members States. In other words an Additional Protocol in force is a condition of supply for the European exports of sensitive items, in particular for the export of enrichment and reprocessing facilities, equipment and technology.

The second condition of supply for trigger list items concerns the submission of four types of *government-to-government assurances*. The first is a commitment of the recipient State to explicitly *exclude any use* which would result in any nuclear explosive device. The second concerns the management of potential retransfer(s). In this regard, suppliers should transfer trigger list items or related technology only upon the recipient's assurance that in the case of retransfer of the concerned items and of items derived from facilities originally transferred, or with the help of equipment or technology originally transferred by the supplier, the recipient of the retransfer or transfer will have to provide the *same assurances as those required by the supplier*

---

9 IAEA, INFCIRC/254/Rev.10/Part 1, Communications Received from Certain Member States Regarding Guidelines for the Export of Nuclear Material, Equipment and Technology, Point 6.

for the original transfer. The third concerns an obligation to bring into force a safeguards agreement requiring the application of safeguards on all trigger list items *if the CSA should be terminated.* The fourth is related to the elaboration of appropriate verification measures or a restitution of transferred and derived trigger list items *if the IAEA decides that an application of IAEA safeguards is no longer possible.*

Complementary to these conditions, suppliers should require from a recipient country to place nuclear material and facilities under effective *physical protection* in order to prevent unauthorised use and handling. The levels of physical protection on which these measures should be based are the subject of an agreement between supplier(s) and recipient(s).

Being specific cases, the transfers of *enrichment and reprocessing facilities, equipment and technology* are submitted to stricter conditions than those applicable to trigger list items. A transfer should not be authorised unless the following conditions are cumulatively met by the recipient State:

- It shall be a *NPT Party* and be in full compliance with its obligations under the Treaty;
- It shall not be identified by an IAEA General Secretariat report as being in breach with its obligations to comply with its safeguards agreement;
- It shall bring into force a Comprehensive Safeguards Agreement and an Additional Protocol (or equivalent regional agreement approved by the IAEA);
- It shall adhere to the NSG Guidelines and report to the UN Security Council that it has implemented effective export controls as identified by UNSCR 1540;
- It shall conclude an inter-governmental agreement with the supplier State including assurances regarding non-explosive use, effective safeguards in perpetuity, and retransfer;
- It shall provide a "legally-binding undertaking (from the recipient State) that neither the transferred facility, nor any facility incorporating such equipment or based on such technology, will be modified or operated for the production of greater than 20% enriched uranium".

Moreover supplier States should encourage recipients to accept, as an alternative to national enrichment and reprocessing facility, *any other appropriate multinational participation* in a resulting facility.

Finally Supplier states should avoid as practicable as it might be a transfer of enabling design and associated manufacturing technology and should negotiate a formal agreement when permitting or enabling replication of the facilities.

Condition of supply for NSG dual-use items

The conditions of supply for dual-use items to be required by the supplier State consists essentially in the submission of three types of government-to-government assurances:

- A statement from the end-user specifying the uses and the end-use locations of the proposed transfers;
- An assurance explicitly stating that the proposed transfer or any replica thereof would not be used in any nuclear explosive active or unsafeguarded nuclear fuel cycle activity;
- An assurance that a prior consent of the supplier will be required before transferring any dual-use item to a State not adhering to the Guidelines.

Criteria for the supply of NSG dual-use items

Different *criteria*, which should be considered in connexion with the non-proliferation principle, are defined for the nuclear dual-use items. These criteria, which are also to be considered for deciding whether or not to grant a licence, are:

(a) Whether the recipient State is a party to the Nuclear Non-Proliferation Treaty (NPT) or to the Treaty for the Prohibition of Nuclear Weapons in Latin America (Treaty of Tlatelolco), or to a similar international legally binding nuclear non-proliferation agreement, and has an IAEA safeguards agreement in force applicable to all its peaceful nuclear activities;

(b) Whether any recipient State that is not party to the NPT, Treaty of Tlatelolco, or a similar international legally-binding nuclear non-proliferation agreement has any facilities or installations listed in paragraph 3(b) above that are operational or being designed or constructed that are not, or will not be, subject to IAEA safeguards;

(c) Whether the equipment, materials, software, or related technology to be transferred is appropriate for the stated end-use and whether that stated end-use is appropriate for the end-user;

(d) Whether the equipment, materials, software, or related technology to be transferred is to be used in research on or development, design, manufacture, construction, operation, or maintenance of any reprocessing or enrichment facility;

(e) Whether governmental actions, statements, and policies of the recipient State are supportive of nuclear non-proliferation and whether the recipient State is in compliance with its international obligations in the field of non-proliferation;

(f) Whether the recipients have been engaged in clandestine or illegal procurement activities; and

(g) Whether a transfer has not been authorised to the end-user or whether the end-user has diverted for purposes inconsistent with the Guidelines any transfer previously authorised; and

(h) Whether there is a reason to believe that there is a risk of diversion to acts of nuclear terrorism.

(i) Whether there is a risk of retransfers of equipment, material, software, or related technology identified in the Annex or of retransfers of any replica thereof contrary to the Basic Principle, as a result of a failure by the recipient State to develop and maintain appropriate, effective national export and transhipment controls, as identified by UNSC Resolution 1540.[10]

The Wassenaar Arrangement (WA)

The Wassenaar Arrangement was established in 1994 after the dissolution of the COCOM in order to contribute to regional and international security and stability.[11] It promotes transparency and greater responsibility in transfers of *conventional arms and dual-use goods and technologies*, with a view to prevent destabilising accumulations. The participating States seek, through their national implementation of the guidelines, to ensure that transfers of these items do not contribute to the development or enhancement of military capabilities that undermine this peace and security, and are not diverted to support such capabilities.

Its objective is to complement and reinforce, without duplication, the existing control regimes for the weapons of mass destruction and their delivery systems as well as other internationally recognised measures. After the terrorist attacks in September 2001, the seventh Wassenaar plenary integrated in the Arrangement's objectives, the prevention of the acquisition of conventional arms and dual-use goods and technologies by terrorist groups and organisations, as well as by individual terrorists.

The decision to effectively transfer or deny a transfer is the sole responsibility of each Participating State. All measures designed in connection with the Initial Elements issued in the frame of the Arrangement are implemented on the basis of national discretion.

---

10 IAEA, INFCIRC/254/Rev.8/Part 2 Communications Received from Certain Member States Regarding Guidelines for Transfers of Nuclear-Related Dual-Use Equipment, Materials, Software and Related Technology, Establishment. of Export Licensing Procedures, Point 4.

11 As of April 2013, 41 countries participate to the Wassenaar Arrangement. Source: http://www.wassenaar.org.

Formally, the Arrangement issues two different sets documents:

- The Initial Elements, which define the purposes, scope, structures and the different procedures set in the framework of the Arrangement;
- The lists of munitions and dual-use goods and technologies, which are reviewed periodically to take into account the technological developments and experience gained.

In July 2004, The Arrangement documents have been formally compiled into one single set of documents called "Guidelines and Procedures, including the Initial Elements".

The Initial Elements

The initial elements define the purposes and the scope of the Arrangement and establish different procedures for information exchanges between the Participating States:

- The *general information exchange* concerns information on risks associated with transfers of conventional arms and dual-use items. The exchanges of information on third States are related to the acquisition activities, export policy, specific project of concern of this State. Since 2003, the exchange of information has been extended to regions where a conflict is occurring;
- The *exchange of information on dual-use goods and technology* deals with the notification of licences for export to third countries which have been denied. The notification contains information on the item, on the country of destination and, for some categories, should mention the reason(s) of the denial.

The notified denial does not impose an obligation on other Participating States to deny the similar transfers. However, a Participating State shall notify – normally within 30 and not later than 60 days – an approval of a licence which has been denied by another Participating States in the three previous years.

The dual-use list

The second pillar of the WA, besides the munitions, is the commitment undertaken by the Participating States to control the transfers, to varying degrees, of the "dual-use" items. This term is not defined by the Initial Elements but should be understood as the items which can be used for both civil and military purposes. The dual-use list consists for a part in a compilation of lists designed by different international export control regimes such as the Missile Technology Control Regime (MTCR), the Australia Group and the NSG.

In addition to these two essential sets of documents, the different Wassenaar Arrangement plenaries have adopted different documents such as best practises, statement of understanding – which delineate more precisely the approach of the different principles contained in the Initial Elements. Some are dedicated specifically to conventional weapons or certain categories of conventional weapons and others concern dual-use goods and, therefore, weapons of mass destruction.

The best practices

The first *non-binding best practices* were adopted by the sixth plenary meeting on extreme vigilance on export control authorisation for some items considered as "highly sensitive".[12][13] For these items, the export authorisation should be granted only on a case-by-case basis. Consultations on the risks of diversion within the exporting country shall be organised between the different competent agencies of the exporting State as to consider the appropriateness of the quantity and the technological level of the item with regard to the stated end-use and the *bona fides* of the end-users. Furthermore, an import certification or an end-user statement, an assurance of no re-export without authorisation and delivery verification certificate or other acknowledgement of delivery from the receiving government shall be required from the recipient before issuing the authorisation. If necessary post-shipment verification should be carried out by the exporter, supplier or other officials of the exporting country.

The second best practises include provisions regarding preventive enforcement, investigations, effective penalties, international cooperation and information exchanges. Participating States shall consider them as sources for an effective national enforcement programme. The penalties as suggested by the best practices should be sufficient to punish and deter violations of export controls and include, as appropriate, criminal sanctions, civil fines, publicity and restriction or denial of export privileges.

The third non-binding best practices[14] intend to establish controls on intangible transfers of technology. The Participating States undertake to think about the definitions of what is an intangible transfer of technology (ITT). Due to the inherent complexity of this problem, the States shall identify the actors in possession of this knowledge, inform

---

12 The items of the "very sensitive list" (sub-set of tier 2). See the dual-use list.

13 These best practices have been adopted by the sixth plenary meeting of the Wassenaar Arrangement (WA) that was held in Bratislava, 30 November-1 December 2000.

14 Agreed at the 2006 plenary session, held in Vienna, 5 and 6 December 2006.

them about the risks associated to dissemination, and promote self-regulation of these actors in order to avoid undesirable transfers. According to these best practices, Participating States may educate the holders of these technologies, as well as the control authorities, to the necessary monitoring of the transfer activities, for example in keeping records of the end-users. Surveillance and appropriate sanctions shall be enhanced by the national authorities and the exchange of information on the various national implementations is promoted.

The fourth non-binding best practices[15] concern the licencing process in the transfer of "basic list" and "sensitive list" items. For practical reasons, the export of these items may be granted through individual but also global and general authorisations, or even licence exceptions – no authorisation application being then required.

Most of the international export control regimes consider now that the industry should play an even more active role in the fight against the WMD proliferation. In this respect, a list of 12 advisory questions have been drafted to give guidance to industry when suspicion is raised and a contact with the national export licencing authorities might be advisable.[16] Furthermore, non binding best practices[17] on the internal compliance programmes (ICP) for industries exporting dual-use goods and technologies has been adopted. It lists essentials elements that industries should consider before exporting sensitive items.

A non-binding list of end use assurance has also been adopted at the fifth plenary of the Arrangement.[18] It contains a list of information that should be contained in the export authorisation application form.

The statements of understanding

The Wassenaar Arrangement has adopted several statements of understanding related to WMD.

The first one, on *intangible transfers of software and technology*[19] provides that a comprehensive export control regime should include controls on transfers of listed "software" and "technology", irrespective of the way in which the transfer takes place. This includes the tangible

15 Agreed at the 2006 plenary session, held in Vienna, 5 and 6 December 2006

16 This list was adopted by the seventh plenary meeting of the Wassenaar Arrangement held in Vienna 10-12 December 2003.

17 Agreed at the 2011 plenary session, held in Vienna, 14 December 2011.

18 The fifth plenary meeting of the Wassenaar Arrangement (WA) was held in Vienna (Austria), 1-3 December 1999.

19 This Statement of Understanding was adopted by the seventh plenary meeting of the Wassenaar Arrangement, held in Vienna, 6-7 December 2001. It has been included in the Control Lists.

transfers of such items but also the intangible transfers of these items, *i.e.* via transmission by electronic media, fax or telephone. Therefore Participating States should include in their national export control, legislation controls on intangible transfers.

The second statement of understanding was dedicated to the *control of non-listed dual-use items* and adopted – without saying it formally – the principle of the "catch-all clause".[20] It requires that Participating States take appropriate measures to ensure that their national legislation requires an authorisation for the transfer of non-listed dual-use items to destinations subject to a (binding) United Nations Security Council arms embargo, any relevant regional arms embargo, either binding or to which a Participating State has voluntarily consented to adhere, when the authorities of the exporting country inform the exporter that the items in question are or may be intended, entirely or in part, for a military end-use. Moreover, if the exporter is aware that the items in question are intended, entirely or in part, for a military end-use, he must notify its suspicion to its national authorities, which will decide whether or not it is adequate to submit the export for authorisation.

The Australia Group (AG)

The governing principles

The initiative to create the Australia Group (AG) was taken after the findings, in April 1984, of the special investigatory mission sent by the UN Secretary General to Iran that chemical weapons had been used in the Iran-Iraq War in violation of the 1925 Geneva Protocol. Moreover, it was evident that Iraq had obtained much of the materials for its chemical weapons programme from the international chemical industry by using the lack of uniformity of national export control systems of the supplying States. Under these circumstances the countries concerned saw an urgent need to address the problem posed by the spread of chemical weapons and ensure that their industries were not, either on purpose or inadvertently, assisting other states to acquire and use such weapons in violation of international law and norms.

This led Australia to propose, in April 1985, that the countries which had introduced licencing obligations for exports might meet in order to examine the scope for harmonising the measures taken individually and

---

[20] This Statement of Understanding was adopted by the seventh plenary meeting of the Wassenaar Arrangement held in Vienna 10-12 December 2003.

for enhancing cooperation amongst them on this issue. The meetings of this informal export control instrument take place, annually, in Paris.[21]

At the beginning of the 1990s, the AG decided to extend its scope of actions against the diversion of dual-use materials to biological weapons programmes. Considering the terrorist attacks in New York in September 2001, the AG has added the prevention against terrorism involving such weapons to its aim of prevention of the acquisition by state actors of chemical and biological weapons (CBW). The objective of AG is thus:

> To ensure, through licencing measures on the export of certain chemicals, biological agents, and dual-use chemical and biological manufacturing facilities and equipment, that exports of these items from their countries do not contribute to the spread of CBW. The Group does this through consultation and harmonisation, thus maximising the effectiveness of participants' national licencing measures. The Group's activities are especially important given that the international chemical and biological industries are a target for proliferators as a source of materials for CBW programs.[22]

The AG considers its activities as complementary to the Chemical Weapons Convention (CWC) and the Biological and Toxin Weapons Convention (BWC), which are the main instruments for addressing the threat posed by chemical and biological weapons.

The export control system

The Australia Group is a soft law instrument which intends to make the measures already taken by participating countries more effective, including through the exchange of information, the harmonisation of legislations and, where necessary, consideration of the introduction of additional national measures. In this respect, the Group has adopted in June 2002 a set of "Guidelines for Transfers of Sensitive Chemical or Biological Items" which should be implemented in the national export control legislations. The first element defined by the Guidelines consists of a list of non-exhaustive *criteria* to take into account the export authorisation decision-making process. These criteria are:

- The consideration of the information at disposal about proliferation and terrorism involving CBW, including any proliferation or terrorism-related activity, or about involvement in clandestine or illegal procurement activities, of the recipient party.

[21] As of April 2013, the Australia Group has 40 Participating States, as well as the European Commission. See http://www.australiagroup.net.

[22] Source: http://www.australiagroup.net/en/objectives.html.

- The consideration of the capabilities and objectives of the chemical and biological activities of the recipient State;
- The review of the appropriateness of the transfer with regard to the stated end-use, including any relevant assurances submitted by the recipient State or end-user and the potential development of CBW;
- The assessment of the end-use of the transfer, including whether a transfer has been previously denied to the end-user, whether the end-user has diverted for unauthorised purposes any transfer previously authorised, and, to the extent possible, whether the end-user is capable of securely handling and storing the item transferred;
- The consideration of the applicability of the relevant multilateral agreements including the BTWC and the CWC.

The transfer should be denied if the supplying government estimates that the items will be used in a chemical or biological weapons programme or for CBW-related terrorism or if there is a significant risk of diversion.

In addition to the review of the criteria, the States should "satisfy themselves" that the items are not intended to be retransferred to a third State. In case of further re-export, the items should be submitted to the Guidelines' principles in the recipient State and the prior consent of the initial exporter should be required. *Government-to-government assurances* confirming such obligation should be exchanged before authorising the first transfer.

The Australia Group has adopted a *no-undercut* mechanism by which an authorisation for an export that is essentially identical to the one denied by another supplier State should only be granted after consultations with this State, provided the delay has not expired or been rescinded. Long debates have been conducted within the Australia group to define precisely what should understand under the terms "essentially identical". A consensus has been reached for considering as essentially identical the transfers of the same biological or chemical agent or in the case of dual-use equipment, the equipment which has the same or similar specifications and performance and with a view to be sold to the same consignee.

Like the others regulation *fora*, the Australia Group has adopted several control lists of items of which transfers shall be submitted for authorisation. However, it remains under the State discretion to apply expedited licencing measures to States which it judges to possess consistently excellent non-proliferation credentials. *Six common control lists* of sensitive items have been adopted for which participating countries have taken the commitment to require export licences. The lists are:

- The chemical weapons precursors list, which contains 54 items;
- The control list of dual-use chemical, manufacturing facilities and equipment and related technology, divided within three groups:
    - Manufacturing facilities and equipment;
    - Toxic gas monitoring systems and detectors;
    - Related technology.
- The list of dual-use biological equipment for export control, divided between "equipment" and "related technology";
- The list of biological agents for export control which contains;
- The core list, with six categories of biological agents (viruses, rickettsiae, bacteria, toxins and subunits, genetic elements and genetically-modified organisms);
- The warning list, with two categories (bacteria, genetically-modified organisms);
- The list of plant pathogens for export controls, containing a core list (divided between bacteria, fungi, genetic elements and genetically-modified organisms) and items for inclusion in awareness-raising guidelines (divided in bacteria, fungi, viruses and genetic elements and genetically-modified organisms)
- The list of animal pathogens for export control, divided in four categories (bacteria, viruses, genetic elements and genetically-modified organisms).

The above lists have been developed during the Australia Group's consultations and are updated as to ensure their continued effectiveness. The difference between a core list and an awareness-raising or warning list remains in the degree of sensitivity of the items, regarding their use in a chemical or biological weapons programme or for CBW terrorism.

In addition to the lists, the Australia Group requires from the States to include in their export control system *two catch-all clauses*. The first requires that an exporter applies for a transfer authorisation of non-listed items when it has been informed by its competent national authorities that the items in question may be intended, in their entirety or part, for use in connection with chemical or biological weapons activities. The second requires that, if the exporter is aware that non-listed items are intended to contribute to WMD activities, it must notify to its national authorities, which will decide whether or not it is expedient to submit the export to an obligation of authorisation.

More recently, the AG has inserted in its Guidelines a provision dedicated to the control of *brokering* transactions. This provision encourages the AG Member States to "have in place or establish measures against illicit activities that allow them to act upon brokering services related to items mentioned in the AG control lists which could contribute to CBW activities".[23]

The Missile Technology Control Regime (MTCR)

Facing the threat that a country could easily divert a peaceful space launch vehicle or another ballistic missile to a nuclear warhead carrier, a group of seven countries decided in 1987 to coordinate their national export licencing efforts to counter the risk of such proliferation.[24] In 1992 the scope of the regime was extended to include missiles capable of delivering biological and chemical – and not only nuclear – weapons.

The principles which govern the Missile Technology Control Regime are contained in the "Guidelines for Sensitive Missile-Relevant Transfers", which appear to have been based on those established by the NSG and those of the former COCOM.[25] The Guidelines form the basis for controlling transfers to any destination beyond the Participating States of WMD delivery systems (other than manned aircraft) and their related equipment and technology. If the missiles submitted to MTCR rules are limited to certain categories defined in terms of payload[26] and range exceeding stated parameters,[27] the Guidelines invite the Participating States to restrain their transfers of any missile, notwithstanding their presence in these parameters. A list of 20 items, divided into two categories, has been adopted and incorporated in the Guidelines' Annex.[28] The transfer of the two items in *category I*[29] are, like those of the NSG "sensitive export", almost forbidden even if the text of the MTCR Guidelines is not expressly that restrictive. Participating States are encouraged to consider transfers of category I items with particular restraint and there "will be a strong presumption to

---

23 Source: http://www.australiagroup.net/en/guidelines.html.

24 As of April 2013, the MTCR has 34 Participating States.

25 Guidelines, list an other relevant documents are accessible at the MTCR web site (http://www.mtcr.info).

26 The total mass that can be carried or delivered by the specified rocket system or unmanned aerial vehicle (UAV) system that is not used to maintain flight.

27 Those parameters are a payload of 500 kg and a range of 300 km.

28 The Guidelines and/or the list have been slightly amended in 1991, 2002 and 2003.

29 Essentially complete systems and subsystems of rockets and unmanned air vehicles with at range of at least 300 km and a delivering capacity of 500 kg payload. Production facilities for these systems are included in category I.

deny such transfer". There is one case of absolute prohibition in the regime, which is the transfer of category I production facilities. In the rare cases where the transfers of the category I items may be authorised, binding government-to-government assurances on end use and the prohibition of retransfer must be required by the exporter. The MTCR Guidelines specify that the suppliers shall "assume responsibility for taking all steps necessary to ensure that the item is put only to its stated end-use".

The transfer of *category II* items is submitted for export authorisation and, when the supplier State "judges on the basis of all available, persuasive information, evaluated according to factors, that they are intended to be used for the delivery of weapons of mass destruction, and there will be a strong presumption to deny such transfers". Factors to be considered by the authorities in their decision-making are:

- The proliferation of weapons of mass destruction in general;
- The capabilities and objectives of the missile and space programmes of the recipient State;
- The significance of the transfer in terms of a potential development of WMD delivery systems;
- The assurances given by the recipient and the applicability of relevant multilateral agreements.

In 2002, considerations of the risk that controlled items fall into the hands of terrorist groups and individuals have been added in the factors contained in the Guidelines.

Similarly to the NSG, a *contamination principle* is also foreseen by the MTCR, which imposes an obligation of prior consent of the supplier for any retransfer not only of the item or the transfer of replicas, but also of the derivatives of the item previously transferred when the transfer could contribute to the delivering of a WMD. The authorisation should be granted only after receiving such assurance from the recipient state, including a statement that the item would be used only for the stated purpose.

In September 2003, a paragraph was inserted in the Guidelines, requiring from the Participating States that they include two *catch-all clauses* in their respective export control systems. The first requires from the exporter that he applies for an authorisation for the transfer of non-listed items where he had been informed by its competent national authorities that the items in question may be intended, in their entirety or part, for use in connection with delivery systems for WMD other than manned aircraft. The second catch-all clause provides that if the exporter is aware that its export of non-listed items is intended to contribute to activities related to the delivery systems of WMD, it must notify its national authorities, which will decide whether or not it is expedient to submit the export for authorisation.

Similar to the other informal non-proliferation instruments, the MTCR, during its annual meeting, reviews its activities and further strengthens its efforts to prevent missile proliferation.

Examples of Implementation

The European Union and the United States

The control of dual-use trade in the European Union

The origins of the system

The first attempt to regulate export control of dual-use items at the EU level was initiated in 1993 due to the necessity of achievement of the European internal market. This objective was put in to practice throughout the adoption of Regulation 3381/94[1] and Joint Action 94/942/CFSP.[2] These legal instruments established the common lists of items to be controlled, authorisation principles and procedures in order to dissuade the proliferators from using potential loopholes in the national legislations of EU Member States. This double set of instruments turned out to be not in conformity with the division of competencies defined by the treaties. In 2000, following two judgments of the Court of Justice of the European Communities confirming the *exclusive competence* of the Communities, the Council adopted Regulation 1334/2000,[3] which compiled the abovementioned legal instruments. This regulation also included several new provisions like the extension of a catch-all clause, and a strengthening of the controls on transfers between the EU Members States. In addition the Council enacted the Joint Action aiming to define a set of common guidelines on the control of technical assistance.[4] These guidelines could not be merged into the Regulation as long as the control of external movement of persons was not in the realm of the EU competence.

---

1 Council Regulation (EC) No. 3381/94 of 19 December 1994 *setting up a Community regime for the control of exports of dual-use goods* (*Official Journal* L 367, 31/12/1994, p. 0001-0007).

2 Council Decision of 19 December 1994 94/942/CFSP on the Joint Action *concerning the control of exports of dual-use goods* (*Official Journal* L 367, 31/12/1994, p. 0001).

3 Council Regulation (EC) No. 1334/2000 of 22 June 2000 *setting up a Community regime for the control of exports of dual-use items and technology* (*Official Journal* L 159, 30/06/2000, p. 0001).

4 Council Joint Action of 22 June 2000 *concerning the control of technical assistance related to certain military end-uses* (2000/401/CFSP) (*Official Journal* L 159, 30/06/2000, p. 0216).

In 2004, the Council, supported by the Commission, launched a peer review process of the Member States' export control regimes. Subsequent to the peer review results, the Commission ordered an impact assessment study on the potential changes to the dual-use Regulation 1334/2000.

After a few years of negotiations within the Council and, later, between the Council and the European Parliament, the Regulation 428/2009[5] recasting the Regulation 1334/2000 and setting up a community regime was adopted under the *co-decision procedure* established by the Lisbon Treaty. The Regulation globally consolidated the commitments of the EU Member States under UNSCR 1540[6] and incorporated a number of provisions on external transit, brokering activities and reviewing or adding certain definitions.

In 2008 the Commission drafted a proposal for a new regulation with view to add the Union's new general export authorisations (EUGEA). This draft regulation was negotiated at the same time as the recast Regulation and was adopted in 2012 (*i.e.* Regulation 1232/2011).[7]

Finally, facing the lengthy process of the co-decision procedure required for the annual update of the list of controlled items defined in the Annex I of the Regulation and of the list of items and destinations to be covered by the EUGEA, the Commission has tabled a proposal to allow for the use of a "delegated acts" procedure to speed up the amending process.[8]

Considering that the successive reforms of the EU export control system within the previous 15 years were designed mostly in reaction to the intra-EU or international constraints, the Commission decided to launch a broad public debate to "identify the strengths and weaknesses of the current system and map out a longer term vision of the EU export control framework". Consequently, in June 2011, it published the *EU*

---

5 Council Regulation (EC) No. 428/2009 of 5 May 2009 setting up a Community regime for the control of exports, transfer, brokering and transit of dual-use items (*Official Journal* L 134, 29/05/2009, p. 0001).

6 United Nations Security Council Resolution 1540 (2004) adopted by the Security Council at its 4956th meeting, on 28 April 2004.

7 Council and Parliament Regulation 1232/2011 of 16 November 2011 amending Council Regulation 428/2009 setting up a Community regime for the control of exports, transfer, brokering and transit of dual-use items (*Official Journal* L 326, 08/12/2011, p. 0026).

8 As of April 2013, this proposition is presently discussed. See the Proposal for a Regulation of the European Parliament and of the Council amending Regulation (EC) No. 428/2009 setting up a Community regime for the control of exports, transfer, brokering and transit of dual-use items (COM(2011) 704 final). Available: http://trade.ec.europa.eu/doclib/docs/2011/november/tradoc_148340.pdf.

Green Paper on the dual-use export system. This consultation took place in the second semester of 2011 and the results thereof published in 2013.[9]

The Regulation 428/2009 as amended by the Regulation 1232/2012 and the Commission Green Paper are the two essential legally binding EU documents referred to when analysing the European dual-use trade control system.

The shape of the system

The legal framework and the competent authorities

The legal framework of the EU export control system is subjected to the division of competencies between the EU institutions and the 27 Member States. As a general principle, the EU does not establish a common export control structure but essentially attempts to coordinate the national regimes of the Member States. The EU and its Member States embody both legislative and implementing authorities even if the EU mainly holds the legislative power and the Member States are, in principle, responsible for the implementing procedures. Although it has been partially opposed by certain Member States, the regulation of transfers of dual-use goods and technology falls within the scope of the Common Commercial Policy, established by the Article 207 of the Treaty on the Functioning of the European Union (TFEU). Therefore, it could not benefit from the Treaty exception[10] as is the case with the weapons trade. The Court of Justice of the Communities – and then of

[9] EU Commission Green Paper (COM(2011) 393 final) *on the dual-use export control system of the European Union: ensuring security and competitiveness in a changing world.* Available: http://trade.ec.europa.eu/doclib/docs/2011/november/tradoc_148340.pdf.

[10] See the exception provided by Article 346 TFEU:

1. The provisions of the Treaties shall not preclude the application of the following rules:

   (a) no Member State shall be obliged to supply information the disclosure of which it considers contrary to the essential interests of its security;

   (b) any Member State may take such measures as it considers necessary for the protection of the essential interests of its security which are connected with the production of or trade in arms, munitions and war material; such measures shall not adversely affect the conditions of competition in the internal market regarding products which are not intended for specifically military purposes.

2. The Council may, acting unanimously on a proposal from the Commission, make changes to the list, which it drew up on 15 April 1958, of the products to which the provisions of paragraph 1(b) apply.

the European Union – has confirmed several times the exclusive competence of the EU in this field.[11]

Taking these remarks into consideration, the EU legal framework regarding dual-use export controls[12] is based on the Council Regulation 428/2009, as amended by Regulation 1232/2011. This Regulation contains the *minimum principles* to be observed by the Member States and offers several *possibilities to adopt more restrictive national policies*.[13] The common elements established by the Regulation are, *inter alia*, a single control list, two mandatory catch-all clauses and the so-called no-undercut principle.

The Member States are wholly responsible for the implementation of the EU law. National authorities implement the entire procedure (including sanctions in compliance with Article 24) and deliver export authorisations (except for the EUGEA, that are under the competence of the Council).

According to the Article 207 TFEU (formerly Article 133 of Treaty on the European Communities, TEC), the common commercial policy and, therefore, the export control policy of dual-use items and technology, shall be conducted with a view to the principles and objectives of the EU external action. These mechanisms are defined by the common foreign and security policy (CFSP) based on Chapter IV of the Treaty on the European Union (TEU) and are consequently implemented following intergovernmental processes. In this regard, the Council has adopted several decisions concerning dual-use export controls and notably the Joint Action 2000/401/CFSP *concerning the control of technical assistance related to certain military end-uses.*[14] This text is considered as a supplement to the Regulation from a legal point of view[15] and covers the cases in which assistance related to chemical, biological or nuclear weapons is provided by an EU resident

---

11 See the European Court of Justice: 17 October 1995 ("Fritz Werner Industrie-Ausrüstungen GmbH v Federal Republic of Germany"), 70/94, Rec. E.C.J., p. 3189 and 17 October 1995 ("Criminal proceedings against Peter Leifer, Reinhold Otto Krauskopf and Otto Holzer"), 83/94, Rec. E.C.J., p. 3231.

12 According to Article 2 of the Council Regulation 428/2009, dual-use items shall mean "items, including software and technology, which can be used for both civil and military purposes, and shall include all goods which can be used for both non-explosive uses and assisting in any way in the manufacture of nuclear weapons or other nuclear explosive devices".

13 See for example Article 4 Paragraph 5 or Article 8 of the Regulation 428/2009.

14 Joint Action 2000/401/CFSP *concerning the control of technical assistance related to certain military end-uses* (*Official Journal* L 159, 30/06/2000, p. 0216).

15 See Article 7 of the dual-use Regulation.

to someone situated in a third country. Such assistance should be either prohibited or authorised.

The specificity of the division of competences between the CCP and the CFSP requires, when the EU considers the implementation of UN Security Council sanctions, the adoption of two legal instruments:[16] a political decision to restrain the trade with a specific State, in the framework of the CFSP, and a legislative act implementing trade restrictions, in the framework of the CCP.[17]

In the field of export control, neither Regulation 428/2008 nor other related regulations or decisions contain the principle of and *extraterritorial application of the European legislation.* Nevertheless, certain Member States might have adopted national provisions meant to apply in other countries or might have implemented a requirement to deliver an authorisation conditioned upon the consent of certain third countries that have directly or indirectly contributed to the development or production of the exported item.[18]

The items covered and procedures

The Annex I of the Regulation 428/2009 contains a *list of dual-use items* that should be submitted for authorisation according to its Article 3. This list is a compilation of various control lists adopted by the international trade control *fora* (*i.e.* the Wassenaar Arrangement, the Missile Technology Control Regime, the Nuclear Suppliers Group, the Australia Group and the Chemical Weapons Convention). The Annex I is divided into ten categories and contains a wide range of items from nuclear materials, facilities and equipment to aerospace and propulsions through computers. This list is regularly updated under the ordinary legislative procedure in conformity with Article 294 TFEU.

---

16 The list of restrictive measures implemented by the European Union can be found at: http://eeas.europa.eu/cfsp/sanctions/docs/measures_en.pdf.

17 For example, when the Council updated the legal framework regarding trade restrictions against Iran at the beginning of 2012 (including restrictions on export of additional dual-use items), two different acts were necessary: the Council Decision 2012/35/CFSP, for the political aspect, and the implementing Council Regulation 56/2012. Both were published in the *Official Journal* (L 29) the same day (24 January 2012).

18 It should be noted that in 1996 the US Congress adopted two acts related to economic restrictions against on the one hand Cuba and Iran and on the other hand Libya. These texts, better known as Helms-Burton and D'Amato acts, provided provisions with extraterritorial effect. Consequently, the EU adopted a Council Regulation and a Joint action (both published in *Official Journal* L 309, 29/11/1996) in order to protect the European industry against the extraterritorial application of legislation adopted by a third country. However, this exception remains specific and does not concern dual-use items and technologies.

Moreover, there are several cases for which an authorisation shall be required despite the fact that the items are not included in the Annex I, under the so-called "catch-all" or "catch more" principle which allows the control of less sensitive dual-use items not listed in Annex I. There exists three catch-all clauses in the dual-use Regulation.

The first catch-all clause allows Member States' competent authorities to require an authorisation for non-listed items *when they have informed the exporter* that these items could contribute to one of the three potential proliferation risks detailed by the Regulation, *i.e.* a potential contribution to the elaboration of an chemical, biological or nuclear weapon; a potential military use in a country subject to an arms embargo; and a potential incorporation in military items that have been previously illegally exported.

The second catch-all clause extends the non-proliferation responsibility to the exporters by constraining them to inform their competent authorities *when they are aware* that the dual-use items which they intend to export could contribute to the elaboration of a WMD or might have a military end-use. After an assessment of the information received from the exporter, the Member State's competent authorities might decide to submit such export for authorisation.

Finally, the Regulation contains an optional catch-all clause allowing Member States to require the exporters to inform them not only when they are aware but also *when they have grounds for suspecting* that the dual-use items which they intend to export might contribute to the elaboration of WMD.

The Regulation, in its Article 8, also enables the Member States to prohibit the export of non-listed items or to submit them for authorisation for reasons of *public security* or *human rights* considerations.

In addition to export transactions, the Regulation 428/2009 addresses brokering, transit and transfers (*i.e.* the movement of goods within the EU). There are no specific controls foreseen for the *impor*t of dual-use items, except those established under the general regime applicable to all import transactions.[19] Moreover, an authorisation delivered by a Member State is valid throughout the EU. The Regulation includes one exception to this principle, for a number of items listed in Annex IV and considered as "highly sensitive". A national transfer authorisation is required for the intra-EU movements of these particular goods, in contradiction with the principle of free movement of goods provided by the Treaty.

---

[19] See Council Regulation (EC) No. 260/2009 of 26 February 2009 *on the common rules for imports*, *Official Journal* L 84, 31/03/2009.

The concept of *brokering* covers a service relation that takes place between two EU third countries while the broker is located within the EU. An authorisation is required if the dual-use items are listed in Annex I and if the national competent authorities have informed the broker or if this one is aware that these items are or may be intended for a WMD-related end-use (Article 5). Although this provision appears to be similar to a catch-all clause, it cannot be considered as such because it refers to the dual-use items listed in Annex I.[20]

A *transit* of non-EU dual-use items listed in Annex I might be prohibited or submitted for authorisation if the dual-use items are or may be intended for a WMD-related end-use. The Member States can extend the authorisation requirement also to non-listed dual-use items or to military items (Article 6 Paragraph 3).

Finally, the Regulation 428/2009 sets a *no-undercut* principle. Before the competent authorities of a Member State grant an authorisation, they should assess all valid denials or decisions to prohibit a transit of dual-use items listed in Annex I that address "essentially identical" transactions. Moreover, they shall consult the competent authorities that have issued the relevant denial or prohibition. If following such consultation an authorisation is nevertheless granted or transit is allowed, the Member States' competent authorities and the Commission are so informed (Article 13).

The different authorisations and criteria

The Regulation establishes three types of authorisations (individual, global and national general) to be delivered by the Member States on a national basis and six authorisations to be delivered by the EU (the European Union export authorisations). These authorisations are valid throughout the European Union.[21]

An *individual export authorisation* is granted to one specific exporter for one specific end-user or consignee situated in a third country and covers one or more dual-use items. A *global export authorisation* covers movements of a type or category of dual-use items to one or more specified end-users situated in one or more specified third countries. A *national general export authorisation* may be used by all national exporters which satisfy the terms and conditions thereof, in order to export to one or more specified end users and for a specific list

[20] The Member States have the possibility to extend the brokering controls to non-listed items which could contribute to the elaboration of WMD and to listed and non-listed items for certain military end-use and specific destinations.

[21] See Article 9 Paragraph 2 of the Regulation 428/2009. The transfers, however, are an exception.

of items. While assessing an export authorisation the national competent authorities should take into consideration four general criteria.[22]

A European Union general export authorisation enables all EU exporters which fulfil certain conditions and requirements to export to several countries. The Regulation 428/2009 establishes six EUGEA. The EU001 – the most "comprehensive" – authorises the exports of dual-use items listed in Annex I to Australia, Canada, Japan, New Zealand, Norway, Switzerland and the United States of America. The five other are object-specific.[23]

The movements within and outside the EU

The European Regulation does not take into consideration the origin of goods or the nationality of industrial operator in order to define in the Member State from which an authorisation shall be required. Except for the transfers of items listed in Annex IV and for those incorporated in the national lists of certain Member States, the dual-use items can move freely from one Member State to another and the export authorisation granted by one Member State is valid throughout the entire EU customs territory. Therefore, once an authorisation is granted the items can leave the EU through any of the EU Member States. The only consideration regarding the location of the item is contained in Article 11 of the Regulation: when the items are located in an other Member State than the one which has issued the export licence, the latter should consult the former which might express a binding objection regarding the authorisation. On the contrary, it seems that the scenario win which the items are located outside the EU and the exporter is established in the EU is not covered by the Regulation. The Member States are consequently free to adopt national provisions concerning this aspect, unless the transaction falls under the scope of brokering provisions set by the Regulation 428/2009.

---

22 Defined in the Article 12 of the Regulation: "The obligations and commitments they have each accepted as members of the international non-proliferation regimes and export control arrangements, or by ratification of relevant international treaties; their obligations under sanctions imposed by a common position or a joint action adopted by the Council or by a decision of the OSCE or by a binding resolution of the Security Council of the United Nations; considerations of national foreign and security policy, including those covered by Council Common Position 2008/944/CFSP of 8 December 2008 defining common rules governing control of exports of military technology and equipment and considerations about intended end-use and the risk of diversion".

23 EUGEA "EU002" relates to export of certain dual-use items to certain destinations; "EU003" to export after repair/replacement; "EU004" to temporary export for exhibition or fair; "EU005" to telecommunications; "EU006" to chemicals.

The same principle can be found in the Joint Action on the control of technical assistance related to certain military end-uses. Its Article 2 provides that "technical assistance shall be subject to controls (prohibition or an authorisation requirement) adopted pursuant to Article 5 where it is provided outside the European Community by a natural or legal person established in the European Community [...]". However, it does not entail that a Member State cannot adopt national provisions based on consideration of citizenship.

The control of dual-use trade in the United States

A control based on a set of provisions

As member – if not initiating – of most of international dual-use export control *fora*, the United States have implemented the related commitments in their legislation and nonetheless preserved national specificities. Indeed, according to the "foreign commerce clause" of the US Constitution[24] and US law, the ability to export dual-use items is considered as a privilege granted to the economic operators and not a right.

At first, the core of the rules governing the export controls of dual-use goods could be found in the Export Administration Act (EAA) of 1979, itself implemented by the Export Administration Regulations (EAR).[25] The EAA expired in 2001 and, since then, the EAR are the main reference.

For historical reasons, the governance of the present US dual-use export control system is assured by several *federal agencies* and is based on various statutory sources. The Bureau of Industry and Security (BIS) of the Department of Commerce authorises the export and re-export of dual-use items and all other items of US origin as long as they are not exclusively regulated by other agencies or exceptionally excluded.[26] The Office of Foreign Assets Controls (OFAC) of the Department of Treasury administers the implementation of the economic embargos and sanctions. The Department of Defence, even though it is not a licencing agency itself, has important reviewing and advising functions. The Department of Energy is competent for the

24 Article 1, Section 8, clause 3 of the Constitution of the United States of America.

25 The Export Administration Act of 1979 (EAA), P.L. 9672 (50 U.S.C. Appendix 2401 and following).

26 The departments of State, Defense and Energy are authorised to review any export licence application submitted to the BIS. The Central Intelligence Agency (CIA) is also authorised to review the licence applications. The agencies will provide BIS with a recommendation to approve or deny the licence application.

licencing of the nuclear technology. The Nuclear Regulatory Commission (NRC) controls the import and export of nuclear materials and equipment.

According to EAR, the obligation of licencing prior to export depends on the item, the final destination, the end-use and the end-user. Some transactions, however, may qualify for one of the 17 licence exceptions, which neutralise the requirement of a licence if the imposed conditions are met. After the licence application is reviewed, the BIS can either approve the application, return it without action[27] or reject it in whole or in part.

The scope of the controls

The EAR regulate in principle the export and re-export of all civil and dual-use items – apart from a few exceptions – with US origin in the United States and worldwide. The export of these items, subsequently, may be controlled through a licencing requirement. As an American specificity, one must note that the US legislation pretends to apply extraterritorially, meaning that not only the export is subjected to the EAR provisions but also the re-export of these items worldwide.[28]

The American regime has also a *list-based* approach. The regulations link the controls to the presence of the item on the Commerce Control List. Nonetheless, non-listed items could also be subject to EAR. These items are designated as belonging to the category "EAR99". They include for example low-technology consumer items, paperclips, perfumes, and toys.

The release of US technology or source code – *i.e.* the executable description of a software system – to a foreign national although *taking place on the US territory* is considered to be a "deemed" export or re-export.[29] These cases are thus covered by the EAR and may be subjected to authorisation requirement. Furthermore, the EAR also regulate *in-country transfers* taking place in a third State if the items of US origin are destined to a prohibited end-user or prohibited end-use. The EAR establish indeed a standardised condition on the re-export submitting

27 "Return without action" means that BIS closes a licence application case without issuing or denying the licence. Such a return may arise notably if the Department of Commerce does not have jurisdiction over the item, if several attempts by BIS to get additional necessary information eventually fail or if the information contained in the application form is inconsistent with the reality of the transaction.

28 Burnett, D.J., "United States of America", in Aubin, Y., Idiart, A. (eds.), *Export Control Law and Regulations Handbook*, Netherlands, 2011, p. 351, 423.

29 EAR, Paragraph 734.2(b)(1) ("deemed export"), Paragraph 734.2(b)(4) ("deemed re-export"). Deemed export and deemed re-export generally follow the same rules as regards the export or re-export of items.

any further resale of the item which export has been authorised by the BIS, including for in-country transfers, to a new approval by the US Government.

The EAR also covers, by a certain "contamination effect", foreign-made items with a certain percentage of "US content". The export of these items, depending on their share of US know-how, may also be controlled. It is called the *de minimis* rule.[30] Furthermore, the EAR regulate the movement of certain entirely foreign-made products if the technology on which these products are based is of US origin.[31] Nationality matters also when it comes to individuals. Some activities of US persons taking place abroad, if they deal with prohibited end-uses, support the proliferation activities or provisions related to embargoes, are subjected to the US export controls.

The US export control system assess the different countries and defines "country groups" with different subcategories, based on the *risk analysis* processed by the federal agencies. Different levels of controls, more or less strict, derive from the ranking in these categories. The levels range over from country group A (usually international *fora* members) to country group E (considered to be sponsors of terrorism), with the most rigorous controls. The destination may also be decisive with regard to the control of non-listed items. A licence may be required in this event when the final destination is an embargoed country,[32] or if the end-use (*e.g.* nuclear end use, even if for maritime propulsion systems, biological or chemical-weapons related) or end-user is of concern for the authorities.[33] The destination – notably when it comes to Iraq, Syria or North Korea[34] – may also be a factor for subjecting the export to licencing requirement under the military end-use related regulations.

---

30 The thresholds amount 10% for shipment to the sponsor□of□terrorism countries Iran, Sudan, Syria, Cuba and North Korea and 25% for shipments to all other countries.

31 "Foreign produced direct product rule". Equally, certain commodities produced by any plant or major component of a plant located outside the United States which are direct product of US origin technology or software, are also subject to US re-export control provisions. See EAR, Paragraph 736.2(b)(3)(ii)(A)(2).

32 Comprehensive licencing requirements exist for shipments of items of US origin to embargoed destinations.

33 EAR, Part 744.

34 EAR, Part 742 paragraph 9 and Part 744 paragraph 19.

What to Control?

The Different Dual-Use Items

The term "items", by essence, is a generic denomination that refers to the field of application of the export controls in general. However, it merely designates "a thing or unit especially included in a list or collection".[1] Particular controls may derive from the specific nature of a subcategory of items. The notions of "goods", "technology" and "software", which are subcategories of the notion of "items" in the dual-use area are thus met in the different export controls regimes and – possibly – defined with view to assigning them rules adapted to their characteristics.

Goods

The notion of "goods", in the dual-use area, is interlinked to the *tangibility* of the items which it refers to. Although technology and software may be transferred in an intangible way, the movement of the goods is exclusively physical. This characteristic affects in a very important way the controls that are effectively applied since, for an export, they are identifiable. They must be carried and conveyed. They tangibly cross borders and customs facilities. They can be physically seized.

In the guidelines provided by the international regimes, the notion of dual-use "goods" is not formally and directly defined. They often make recourse to the term "items" even for designating the tangible ones, which formally constitute the sub-category of the "goods". The non-proliferation treaties addressing the issues connected to weapons of mass destruction, which are at the basis of these regimes, do not even use these notions. Furthermore, it must be noted that these references and mentions are always "purposive" in the meaning that their field of application is bound to the scope of the regime.

The Non-Proliferation Treaty, in its Article III.2, does not mention any of the terms but only the "equipment and materials" which can serve proliferation purposes. The Biological and Toxin Weapon Convention[2] and the Chemical Weapon Convention[3] do not refer to these terms either but, respectively, to "the agents, toxins, weapons,

---

1 Source: Collins English Dictionary.

2 Article III.

3 Article I.

equipment or means of delivery specified in article I of this Convention" and the "chemical weapons and related activities", as being the scopes of their application.

The *fora* that develop the provisions contained in these conventions have defined their own boundaries though detailing the notions. The Zangger Committee[4] designates under the term "items" "equipment or material especially designed or prepared for the processing, use or production of special fissionable material".

The Australia Group refers to "the materials, equipment, technology and software that could contribute to CBW activities", thus suggesting that the sub-category of "goods" may be further divided between "materials" and "equipment". However, the control list adopted by this *forum* only refers – without defining it – to the "equipment".

The Nuclear Suppliers Group[5] adopts "Guidelines for transfers of nuclear-related dual-use equipment, materials, software and related technology", the title of which comforting the interpretation proposed through the observation of the Australia Group's guidelines. Even though the NSG does not propose a formal definition of the "equipment" and "materials", it characterises them with the scope of application of the controls it prescribes. It states that it targets such equipment and materials that "could make a major contribution to a "nuclear explosive activity," an "unsafeguarded nuclear fuel-cycle activity" or acts of nuclear terrorism".[6]

Other international regimes, finally, do not operate the same classification. In the Resolution 1540(2004), "items" refer to "materials" related to the "proliferation of nuclear, chemical, or biological weapons and their means of delivery"[7] as well as the aforementioned weapons and their means of delivery. In the guidelines of the Missile Technology Control Regime, the terms "items" and "equipment" are indifferently used but they are opposed to "technology". "Items" and "goods", here, are conceptually merged. The Wassenaar Arrangement uses the term "goods" in the title of its Initial Elements[8] and the section dedicated to

---

4 IAEA, INFCIRC/209/Rev.2, Communications of 15 November 1999 Received from Member States Regarding the Export of Nuclear Material and of Certain Categories of Equipment and other Material, Memorandum B, Paragraph 2.

5 IAEA, INFCIRC/254/Rev.8/Part.2, Communication Received from Certain Member States Regarding Guidelines for Transfers of Nuclear-related Dual-Use Equipment, Material, Software and Related Technology.

6 *Ibid.*, Paragraph 1.

7 UNSC Resolution 1540(2004), Paragraph 3.

8 Wassenaar Arrangement on Export Controls for Conventional Arms and Dual-Use Goods and Technologies, Guidelines & Procedures, including the Initial Elements, December 2011.

the scope of its controls. However, it does not provide any definition of it.[9]

In the United-States' internal regulations,[10] the term "goods" is not used. However, according to the definitions provided[11] an "item" means "commodities, software, and technology". The term "commodity" is thus used instead of "goods", as a sub-category of "items" existing beside "technologies" and "software". The same paragraph even provides a definition of the "commodity" in this acceptance: "any article, material, or supply except technology and software". The Regulations[12] states that, in order to be subjected to the controls, the status of the "item of activity" shall be reviewed with the light of the Commerce Control List and the provisions of the Regulations.

The European Union Regulation 428/2009,[13] in its Article 2, proposes a comprehensive definition of the "items", which it refers to in the title of the Regulation notably. According to its wording, the dual-use items, including technology and software, are the items that "can be used for both civil and military purposes, and shall include all goods which can be used for both non-explosive uses and assisting in any way in the manufacture of nuclear weapons or other nuclear explosive devices". The Regulation thus proposes a definition of the "dual-use" characteristic, not making any distinction between used and new items, rather than a proper definition of the term "items" and does not define the "goods" in this picture. The expression "goods", indeed, is only referred to in a generic way in the Regulation but is not aimed at discriminating – with a view to the application of controls – "goods" *stricto sensu* from technology of software. This definition of the dual-use items by the European Union cumulates the "purposive" understandings of this term since it first refers to military and non-military purposes, *i.e.* the Wassenaar Arrangement, the Australia Group and the MTCR definitions, and then refers to nuclear and non-nuclear purposes, *i.e.* the NSG definition. Similar to these international and national regimes mentioned above, the European Regulation sets a list of items to which the controls apply. However, this "written" reference for characterising an item as a dual-use one is mitigated by the possible

---

9 The Wassenaar Arrangement has published, in its List of Dual-Use Goods and Technologies and Munitions List (WA-LIST(12) 1 of 12 December 2012), a section dedicated to the "Definition of terms used in these lists".

10 Export Administration Regulations (EAR).

11 EAR, Title 15, Paragraph 772.1.

12 EAR, Title 15, Paragraph 734.2.

13 Council Regulation (EC) No. 428/2009 of 5 May 2009 *setting up a Community regime for the control of exports, transfer, brokering and transit of dual-use items* (*Official Journal* L 134, 29/05/2009), hereafter referred to as "the Regulation".

application, under most of the international *fora*, of catch-all provisions. In a general way, therefore, the definition of "items", "goods", but also "technology" and "software" as dual-use ones is subjected to both aspects of principle and opportunity.

As an example of the implementation of the European provisions, it must be noted that in the French system, the words "goods" and "items" are translated with the same word (*biens*). The distinction between the category and the sub-category thus cannot be operated. The French texts do not attempt to specify the European definitions. They merely add new "items"-"goods" such as helicopters and their spare elements as well as tear gas and riot control agents to the scope of the dual-use export controls. Furthermore, the French regulations do not operate the distinction between "items"-"goods" and "technology" or "software", either. The French system is comprehensive and legally subjects all these sub-categories to the same regime and controls.

Technology

As regards the definition of "technology", one may state from the analysis of the most prominent international – or national – prescriptions, that there is a large consensus on the meaning of the term when it is used. The definitions found are the same from an international *forum* to an other. The NSG – for both the trigger list and the dual-use items –, the MTCR in the annex of its Guidelines and the Wassenaar Arrangement in its *Guidelines & Procedures, including the Initial Elements*, have adopted exactly the same definition. In the systems they set, "technology" means "specific information required for the "development", "production", or "use" of any item (dealt with by the *forum*). This information may take the form of "technical data", or "technical assistance"". They also have the same definitions for the *technical data*, which "may take forms such as blueprints, plans, diagrams, models, formulae, engineering designs and specifications, manuals and instructions written or recorded on other media or devices such as disk, tape, read-only memories", and for the *technical assistance*, which "may take forms such as: instruction, skills, training, working knowledge, consulting services".

Furthermore, all these regimes limit the boundaries of the targeted "technology" to exclude information in the "public domain" and "basic scientific research" products, these notions being defined hereafter. In the definition it provides, the Wassenaar Arrangement also specifies the note and lists in which the characteristics of the controlled technology can be found.

The United States' national Regulations[14] reproduce the same definitions and include a similar reference to the notes and lists

Although the technology is controlled because listed in a first place, the catch-all provisions do apply to technology as well.

In its Annex I, the European dual-use Regulation provides a definition of technology that is similar to the definition provided by the other international systems. The General Technology Note, the Nuclear Technology Note and the General Software Note of the same annex exempt from export authorisation any technology which derives from the public domain or is necessary for the basic scientific research or – only for items other than "nuclear materials, facilities and equipment" – the minimum necessary information for patent application. Technology of the *public domain* should be understood as a technology available without any restrictions upon further dissemination (a copyright does not remove technology from the public domain). Technology of the *basic scientific research* means experimental or theoretical work undertaken principally to acquire new knowledge of the fundamental principles and of phenomena or observable facts which are not primarily directed towards a specific practical aim or objective. It must be emphasised also that an authorisation covers the minimum technology necessary for the installation, operation, maintenance and repair of the items supplied if it provides operating instructions and some basic specifications, similar to the technical manual or user's guide supplied with machines of the everyday life.

The technical assistance, although it is not directly incorporated in a product but is a component of the dual-use "know-how", must be brought close to technology with regard to its export control conditions. The Joint Action 2000/401/CFSP[15] completes the European export control system as regards technical assistance for certain items with a military end-use, in providing an extensive definition of the term. Article 1 of the Joint Action defines this assistance as "any technical support related to repairs, development, manufacture, assembly, testing, maintenance, or any other technical service, and may take forms such as instruction, training, transmission of working knowledge or skills or consulting services". It may include "oral forms of assistance".

Despite the existence of a definition at the European level, one may note that some Member States have inserted a definition of "technology" in their national implementing legislation. In the British

---

[14] EAR, Title 15, Paragraph 772.

[15] Council Joint Action of 22 June 2000 (2000/0401/CFSP) *concerning the control of technical assistance related to certain military end-uses* (*Official Journal* L 159, 30/06/2000).

Export Control Order,[16] technology means information (including but not limited to information comprised in software and documents such as blueprints, manuals, diagrams and designs) that is "capable of use in connection with the development, production or use of any goods". It is interesting to note, here, that the United-Kingdom has left some room for controlling technology that would be only "capable" – and not compulsorily "necessary"[17] – to be used for such purposes, which enlarges the possibilities of controls.

Software

Similar to the definition of "technology", the same definition of "software" can be found in the dual-use export control systems and regimes "worldwide". The dual-use list of the NSG, the annex of the MTCR guidelines, the *Guidelines & Procedures, including the Initial Elements* of the Wassenaar Arrangement all provide the same definition, indeed: "a collection of one or more "programs" or "microprograms" fixed in any tangible medium of expression".

The United-States internal Regulations[18] provide exactly the same definition and so does the European Regulation in its Annex I. In the General Software Note of the same annex, nonetheless, the European Union excludes from the definition, and the scope of application of the controls therefore, the software for all categories of items of the list which are generally made available to the public by being sold from stock at retail selling points or designed for installation by the user without substantive support from the supplier,[19] as well as the software containing information in the public domain.

As an example of the national implementation of the European provisions, the United-Kingdom, in its Export Control Order 2008, has reproduced the international and European definition in its legislation.

---

[16] Export Control Order 2008, Part 1, Paragraph 2.

[17] Some international systems mentioned above use the term "required", the American EAR and the European Regulation use the term "necessary", which has the same strength.

[18] EAR, Title 15, Paragraph 772.1.

[19] An exception to the exemption is set, nevertheless, for software of the "telecommunication and information security" category (5) which are related to "information security". For this specific software, the controls apply in all situations.

The Controlled Movements

In the domain of export control, the term "export" often goes beyond the mere cross-border flows of goods. It rather reflects the idea of movement that lies behind, although the term "movement" is even more generic and also encompasses aspects of transport, or even speculation on the good. The movements controlled by the different legal acts and regimes define the scope of application of the guidelines they edit. Exports, transfers, re-exports, transit, transhipment, brokering and technical assistance are the most important that are shaped and, sometimes, formally defined by the applicable rules and regimes.

Export and transfer

The observation of the different international systems, the European and some national ones, reveals that the terms "export" and "transfer" are often used as synonymous. However, this is not true of every regime. Furthermore, they may be used to reflect more than their narrow meaning suggests.

First, transfer can be used for designating the whole range of movements controlled by an act or a regime. Originally, the NPT used the terms "provision" and "international exchange"[1] without defining them further, to refer to the movements it seeks to include in its scope. The BTWC, the Wassenaar Arrangement and the MTCR address the "transfers"[2] of the goods and technologies they control. The Australia Group[3] develops the notion a bit further in stating that these transfers may be tangible or intangible.

Then, it can be noticed that "export" and "transfer" can be used as synonymous and for designating a selection of movements controlled, including the narrow meaning of "export". The global reading of the legal act or the regime's guidelines allows for defining whether the use of the word "export/transfer" corresponds to a generic or a more restricted – though not limited to the narrow definition – meaning. In these cases, either term is used in opposition to other vocabularies

1 Articles III.2 and III.3, respectively.

2 See for examples: BTWC Article III, Wassenaar Arrangement Initial Elements, Paragraph II, MTCR Guidelines Paragraph 1.

3 See Australia Group Guidelines, Paragraph 1.

referring to different movements, such as "import" in the CWC,[4] "retransfer" in the NSG Guidelines for Nuclear Transfers[5] and in the Zangger Committee's guidelines.[6]

As regards a clear distinction between export and transfer, the international regimes give little certainty. The Australia Group,[7] the MTCR,[8] the Wassenaar Arrangement[9] and the NSG[10] most often use the term "transfer" to refer to the movement but use the term "export" when referring to "export legislations" or "export controls" as a legal and administrative domain in general.

The Wassenaar Arrangement's guidelines open the way for a second interpretation. The Initial Elements include in the same time references to the "transfers of conventional arms and dual-use goods and technologies"[11] and to the "exports of arms and sensitive dual-use goods".[12] Therefore, the question may legitimately be asked whether the technology would not be the differentiating element of the definitions of "exports" and "transfers". This is however not confirmed by any international regimes or legal acts other than the Wassenaar Arrangement.

Not only the international *fora* follow this holistic approach encompassing several movements under one single term. National legislations like the French or the American ones do so as well. Others, like the Japanese legislation, follow the distinction set from the reading of the Wassenaar Arrangement between the "transfer" meant for technologies and "exports" meant for the goods. In the French regulations, all movements controlled are in principle referred to as "exports" in opposition to imports.[13] Therefore, re-exports, transit, transhipment and brokering, for example, are dealt with through "export" procedures.

---

4 CWC Part VII, Paragraph 8.

5 IAEA, INFCIRC 254/rev10/Part1, Guidelines for Nuclear Transfers, Paragraph 1.

6 IAEA, INFCIRC/209/rev2, Consolidated Trigger List, Memorandum A, Paragraph 4 and Memorandum B, Paragraph 4.

7 See for example: Australia Group Guidelines, paragraphs 3 to 5.

8 See for example: MTCR Guidelines, Paragraph 7.

9 See for example: Initial Elements, Paragraph VII.

10 IAEA, INFCIRC 254/rev10/Part1, Guidelines for Nuclear Transfers and IAEA, INFCIRC 254/rev8/Part2, Guidelines for Transfers of Nuclear-Related Dual-Use Equipment, Materials, Software and Related Technology.

11 See for example: Initial Elements, Paragraph I.1.

12 See for example: Initial Elements, Paragraph IV.2.

13 Décret n°2001-1192 du 13 décembre 2001 *relatif au contrôle à l'exportation, à l'importation et au transfert de biens et technologies à double usage.*

In the American Export Administration Regulations (EAR) – which are together one of the rare acts actually providing a definition of the notion – export is defined as "an actual shipment or transmission of items subject to the EAR out of the United States, or release of technology or software subject to the EAR to a foreign national in the United States".[14] This definition not only vary from the common acceptance of the cross-border characteristic of an export, since the nationality is an alternative criteria to the location, but it also includes "activities other than exports",[15] such as technical assistance cases or cases of transit or transhipment.[16] The EAR also establish, as an exception to the regime of the "classical" exports, specific controls and licences for "temporary exports" of items temporarily located in the United States and of beta test software.[17]

Finally, the terms "transfer" and "export" can be used for designating one activity only. In the UNSC Resolution 1540(2004),[18] the "export" is clearly distinguished from transit, transhipment, re-export and other "services related to such export". However, the Resolution uses the two terms – "transfer" and "export" – alternatively, as synonymous.

The European dual-use Regulation[19] is unique in the sense that it makes a conceptual difference between these two, even in the title of the Regulation. Point 12 of the Preamble and Article 22 establish that the transfer is a movement of an item or a technology *inside the European Union* territory contrary to the export, defined at Article 2.2, which concerns goods "leaving the Community customs territory" and includes also the re-exports and intangible movements of technology. The term "export", therefore, *covers the re-export* in the European definition, although the latter one is a separate activity in most of the international and in some national regimes. The European regime thus follows, somehow, a holistic approach too.

---

14 Export Administration Regulations, Title 15, Paragraph 734.2 "Scope of the EAR".

15 Export Administration Regulations, Title 15, Paragraph 730.5 "General information", Point (c).

16 Export Administration Regulations, Title 15, Paragraph 734.2 "Scope of the EAR", Point (k).

17 Export Administration Regulations, Title 15, Paragraph 740.9 "Temporary imports, exports and re-exports (TMP)".

18 UNSC Resolution 1540(2004), Article 3 (d).

19 Council Regulation (EC) No. 428/2009 of 5 May 2009 setting up a Community regime for the control of exports, transfer, brokering and transit of dual-use items (*Official Journal* L 134, 29/05/2009), hereafter referred to as "the Regulation".

Re-export and re-transfer

The international *fora* provide little indication with regard to a definition of the re-export movement despite the fact that they all stress the singularity of this form of movement with regard to simple exports. The Resolution 1540 expressly organises controls of the re-exports[20] as well as the other systems do, through different names however. The Australia Group,[21] the Zangger Committee,[22] the MTCR[23] and the NSG[24] guidelines use the term "re-transfer", and the Wassenaar Arrangement the term "subsequent transfer".[25] The re-export, in the absence of formal definition, shall thus be understood as the transfer from a country of destination of an item or technology to a new country of destination, which was *not foreseen at the time of the export*. These different systems generally set an obligation for the importer to provide assurances that the item or technology will not be re-exported unless the consent of the primary supplier is obtained. The MTCR and the NSG[26] complete the scope of the "re-exports" in adding the transfer of any replica of the good that was primarily exported.

The European Regulation recognises the re-exports as a distinct movement, in principle, from the exports, as demonstrated by the preamble.[27] However, they are formally assimilated to exports in the definition provided at Article 2.2 of the Regulation.

In the United States, the exports and re-exports are generally on the same footage with regard to the prohibitions[28] or the licence exceptions,[29] meaning that their legal regimes are similar. This is valid also with regard to temporary re-exports,[30] which are aligned to the authorisation regime that corresponds to the temporary exports. Nevertheless, the EAR provide a specific definition of the re-exports, distinct from the exports: "an actual shipment or transmission of items

20 Article 3 (d).

21 Paragraph 5.

22 Paragraph 5.

23 Paragraph 5.

24 IAEA, INFCIRC/254/rev10 Part 1, Paragraph 9 and IAEA, INFCIRC/254/rev8 Part 2, Paragraph 7.

25 Wassenaar Arrangement, "Best Practice Guidelines on Subsequent Transfer" (Re-Export) Controls of Conventional Weapon System Contained in Appendix 3. The Initial Elements, however, use the term "re-transfers" (*e.g.* at Paragraph III.1).

26 MTCR Guidelines, Paragraph 5 and IAEA, INFCIRC/254/rev8 Part 2, Paragraph 7.

27 Regulation 428/2009, Preamble, Point 12.

28 EAR, Title 15, Part 736 "General prohibitions".

29 EAR, Title 15, Part 740 "License exception".

30 EAR, Title 15, Part 740, Paragraph 9.

subject to the EAR from one foreign country to another foreign country; or release of technology or software subject to the EAR to a foreign national outside the United States".[31]

Transit

As regards transit in the international acts and control systems, only the Resolution 1540 makes clear reference to it,[32] though it does not define the notion.

According to the Article 2.7 of the European Regulation, transit shall mean "a transport of non-Community dual-use items entering and passing through the customs territory of the Community with a destination outside the Community". Contrary to the United States' regime, the item is not considered to have a European origin automatically because of its location on the European customs territory and the transit thus defined takes place on this European territory. The wording of the Article 2.7 is relatively extensive and has predisposed Member States to implement "transit procedures" to a wide range of scenarios with items remaining on board or items which are unloaded or transhipment or cases where means of transport are to be changed.[33]

In the French system, which follows a holistic approach, there is no such "transit procedure" and the authorisations must follow a standard "export procedure". However, the reality of transit – and brokering – is acknowledged since, in the application forms,[34] the exporters must state the countries of origin, of departure and of destination of the goods and may be required to provide additional information on these intermediaries and on the nature of the movement to the authority. In addition, outside the sphere of the dual-use goods, there exists in the French regime[35] an obligation to submit the "direct transit from border to border, by road, of listed materials, arms and ammunitions" for a prior authorisation.

The American EAR consider "transit" through a totally different perspective. They do not define it either but set, as a general prohibition, provisions concerning the transit through foreign countries. The general prohibition number 8,[36] indeed, establishes that transit through a country

---

31 EAR, Title 15, Part 734, Paragraph 2 (k).

32 Article 3 (d).

33 Michel, Q., "The European Union Dual-Use Items Control Regime: Comment of the Legislation: article-by-article", June 2012, p. 23.

34 See for example the French application form CERFA 10994-03 "Dual-use items export".

35 Code de la Défense, Article R.2335-41

36 EAR, Title 15, Part 736, Paragraph 8.

specifically listed may not take place without a licence exception or a licence authorising an export or re-export to this country of transit. It also states that "for purposes of the EAR, the export or re-export of items subject to the EAR that will transit through a country or countries or be transhipped from a country or countries to a new country or are intended for re-export to the new country, are deemed to be exports to the new country".[37] The regime the EAR shape, therefore, does not deal with transit through the United States, as the European provisions do for the EU or Member States' territories, but sets obligations concerning transit through foreign countries.

Transhipment

The international export control *fora* do not set particular procedures as regards transhipment of sensitive goods, which consists under the common sense definition in the change of the export's means – *i.e.*, transport or packaging – on their way to their final destination. The Resolution 1540[38] recognises the particularity and importance of "transhipment" controls in opposition to "export" controls but it does not formally define the term. The NSG Guidelines[39] acknowledges the necessity to establish transhipment controls beside export controls but they do not elaborate nor define their guiding principles.

The American EAR do not provide any legal definition of transhipment either but they set a specific regime for it similar to the transit,[40] described above. Transhipment controls, therefore, target transhipments in other countries and are assimilated to "simple" exports.

In the European Regulation, transhipment regime is not aligned on "exports" but on "transit", from which it is not formally singled out. There is no specific control on transhipment movements, nor any definition made available. However, European Union Member States, while implementing the European rules, may decide to apply transit procedures to transhipment.[41] As an example, the French dual-use legislation does not contain any specific definition or regime for transhipment. However, it does make a specific case of the transhipment in the French seaports and airports of an import to France of listed materials, arms and ammunitions. In this case, the transhipment must be authorised under the form of a transit authorisation, as described in the

37 EAR, Title 15, Part 734, Paragraph 2(m).

38 Article 3(d).

39 IAEA, INFCIRC/254/rev10 Part 1, Paragraph 9 and IAEA, INFCIRC/254/rev8 Part 2, Paragraph 4.

40 EAR, Title 15, Part 736, Paragraph 8 and EAR, Title 15, Part 734, Paragraph 2 (m).

41 Michel, Q., *op. cit.*, p. 23.

related section, for these sensitive goods.[42] On the contrary, the United-Kingdom Export Control Order 2008 provides a definition. The term designates "transhipment with a view to the re-exportation of the goods or a transhipment of the goods for use as stores".[43] If the movement of dual-use items is aimed at certain destinations or if it does not meet three cumulative conditions, the transhipment is submitted for specific prior authorisation through open general transhipment licences (OGTL, four types) or standard individual transhipment licences (SITL).[44]

Brokering

"Brokering" is relatively often considered and dealt with by the international export control regulations. In the Resolution 1540, the States are required to act again the "illicit trafficking and brokering"[45] of WMD-related material in developing and maintaining effective national controls on the "services" related to the export and transhipment of these goods,[46] thus making again a clear connection to brokering activities.

The Australia Group Guidelines do not define the "brokering" in the dedicated – final – section but they state that the role of the brokers in the transfer must be taken into account as factors by the authorities when deciding to grant the licence.[47] Furthermore, they contain a dedicated paragraph, titled "Brokering services", which obliges the members to include in the scope of their legislations and practices the brokering activities, as they can contribute to activities prohibited under the CWC and BTWC.

The Wassenaar Arrangement has set particular provisions for the brokering activities in its "Elements for Effective Legislation on Arms Brokering". It defines the brokering as "activities of negotiating or arranging contracts, selling, trading or arranging the transfer of arms and related military equipment controlled by Wassenaar Arrangement Participating States from one third country to another third country".[48] It consequently sets an obligation for the Member States to establish by

---

42 Code de la Défense, Article R.2335-1.

43 Export Control Order 2008, Part 1 Paragraph 2.

44 Review of Export Control Legislation (2007) Supplementary Guidance Note on Trade "Transit and Transhipment" Controls, Department fro Business, Innovation and Skills, March 2012, paragraphs 4.2, 4.3, 5.1, 5.2.

45 Article 3 (c).

46 Article 3 (d).

47 Paragraph 4 (d).

48 Wassenaar Arrangement, "Elements for Effective Legislation on Arms Brokering", agreed at the 2003 plenary, Paragraph 1.

legislation and regulations a regime of authorisation of these activities and gives the right to the States to further define the brokering as to "include cases where the arms and military equipment are exported from their own territory".[49] The regime of brokering activities thus depends on the practices of the different Participating States. It goes even further in setting a regime for the brokers themselves, which it defines as "citizens, residents of otherwise subject to the jurisdiction of the State",[50] in allowing the States to limit the number of brokers authorised to exercise their activity[51] and establish a register of the brokers.[52]

The United States EAR do not specifically address brokering activities as regards dual-use goods. However, if they are exercised in relation with "military commodities", they are to be found under the licencing jurisdiction of the Department of State.[53]

The EU Regulation brings another definition of the brokering services, which details the definition provided for by the Wassenaar Arrangement. Under the Article 2.5, they shall mean "the negotiation or arrangement of transactions for the purchase, sale or supply of dual-use items from a third country to any other third country; or the selling or buying of dual-use items that are located in third countries for their transfer to another third country", excluding ancillary services.[54] In the Article 5, the Regulation sets a regime of authorisation for such activities, if the broker has been informed by its authorities or is aware that the good may serve proliferation purposes. Notwithstanding this formal resemblance with the catch-all mechanism, one must note that it gives the possibility to submit for prior authorisation requirements activities related to listed articles, and not to non-listed articles such as in catch-all provisions.

The United Kingdom extended the scope of its controls over brokering activities to transactions that are normally not accounted as European ones, for example if a broker normally established in the United Kingdom is organising the transaction from outside EU territory.[55]

---

49 *Idem.*

50 *Idem.*

51 *Idem.*

52 *Idem*, Paragraph 2.

53 EAR, Title 15, Part 774 "Commerce Control List".

54 "Ancillary services" under the Article 2.7 are services of transportation, financial services, insurance or re-insurance or general advertising or promotion.

55 United Kingdom Export Control Order 2008, Article 11.

Technical assistance

As regards the international instruments, few of them define and/or regulate the activities of the technical assistance. The Resolution 1540 is comprehensive in the sense that it covers "services related to [...] the exports and transhipments",[56] which implicitly include the technical assistance services. However, it does not define their scope. It only contains the obligation for the States to establish controls on the supply of this assistance.

The NSG provides more details on the notion. In the annexes of the guidelines,[57] "technology" is defined as "the specific information required for the development, production or use of any item of the list(s)" and includes the technical assistance, which is a form of "technology" and must therefore be controlled as an intangible movement. Technical assistance is further described as multiform, given the fact that it includes aspects "such as instruction, skills, training, working, knowledge, consulting services and may involve technical data".[58]

The United States EAR make the same connection between "technology" and "technical assistance". Indeed, according to the Commerce Control List's section on "technology", "when a person performs or provides technical assistance that incorporates, or otherwise draws upon, "technology" that was either obtained in the Unite States or is of US-origin, then a release of "technology" takes place".[59] An authorisation may thus be required.

According to the Article 2.2 or the Regulation, the European Union considers the following content as "export":

> (The) transmission of software or technology by electronic media, including by fax, telephone, electronic mail or any other electronic means to a destination outside the European Community; it includes making available in an electronic form such software and technology to legal and natural persons and partnerships outside the Community. Export also applies to oral transmission of technology when the technology is described over the telephone.

It expressly covers technology and cases of technical assistance as they are defined by the NSG. However, under its Article 7, the

---

56 Article 3 (d).

57 IAEA, INFCIRC/254/rev10 Part 1, Annex A and IAEA, INFCIRC/254/rev8 Part 2, Annex A.

58 According to the same annexes, "technical data", themselves, "may take different forms, such as blueprints, plans, diagrams, models, formulae, engineering designs and specifications, manuals and instructions written or recorded on other media or devices such as disk, tape, read-only memories".

59 EAR, Title 15, Part 774 "Commerce Control List", 5E002.

Regulation does not apply to the supply of services or the transmission of technology if that supply or transmission involves the cross-border movement of persons. Eventually, all dual-use technical assistance scenarios are not covered, and those that are covered shall be understood as and follow the regime of an export.

As regards the goods related to certain military end-use, the Joint Action 2000/0401/CFSP[60] addresses specifically the technical assistance activities which concern many of the dual-use items covered by the Regulation. It defines, in its Article 1, the technical assistance as the "technical support related to repairs, development, manufacture, assembly, testing, maintenance, or any other technical service, which may take forms such as instruction, training, transmission of working knowledge or skills or consulting services", including oral forms of assistance. Cross-border movements of persons are, here, considered but not the transfers of information that is in the public domain or basic scientific research. Beside this definition, the Joint Action establishes[61] the obligation for the European Union Member States to establish controls – through a regime of prohibition or prior authorisation – of the technical assistance services provided by a EU supplier to a third-country entity when these services are in connection with WMD or their means of delivery. These controls involve also the possibility of the application of catch-all mechanisms on technical assistance provided to third countries if it is intended, or the provider is aware that it is intended for:

- A WMD-related end use (Article 2); or
- A military end use in countries of destination subject to an arms embargo (Article 3).

It should be emphasised that the principles of the Joint Action must be transposed in the national legislations of the EU Member States in order to acquire a legally binding effect.

The intangible transfers

The necessity to control the transfers – in their broad meaning – of *intangible* technology (ITT) became recently one of the main concerns of the international community even if they are not ruled formally by international trade control *fora* like it is for export or, more recently, brokering transactions. Only the Wassenaar Arrangement adopted at the

---

60 Council Joint Action of 22 June 2000 (2000/0401/CFSP) *concerning the control of technical assistance related to certain military end-uses* (*Official Journal* L 159, 30/06/2000).

61 Article 2.

2006 plenary a set of *Best Practices for Implementing Intangible Transfer of Technology.*[62] These best practices encourage the States to adopt dedicated legislation controlling the movements of intangible technology, in two ways.

First, they shall define what constitutes an ITT. Unfortunately, the document does not propose a definition, nor tools to support its elaboration. Only the term "technology" has been comprehensively defined by the Wassenaar Arrangement as well as by most international export control *fora.*[63] For these regimes it shall include specific information that is necessary for the development, production or use of a controlled item and it could take the form of technical data or technical assistance.[64]

Then, the WA Best Practices invite the States to define within their national legislation the intangible technology transfers subject to controls. Similar to the definition, the document did not go further than establishing the principle and the other international export control instances did not include dedicated provisions on the transactions to be submitted for export authorisation. Nevertheless, the situation is not fundamentally different to the one applicable to tangible transfers: none of the export control regimes describes export, import or brokering further than the principle to submit those transactions for export control. It belongs to States to implement this principle, keeping in mind that, globally, the "online" world should be controlled in the same proportionate manner as the "offline" one. Therefore, the implementation can take the form of an export authorisation or a prohibition to export or a mix of both.

The EU export control regime constitutes an interesting example of this dual approach. The Regulation 428/2009 submits for authorisation the transfers of controlled technology by tangible and by intangible forms without distinction. No specific instrument has been established to control intangible transfers and they could benefit also from the EUGEA. Some EU Member States grant global authorisations for ITT to certain exporters. Intangible transfers through cross-border movement

62 This document is available on the Wassenaar Arrangement website: http://www.wassenaar.org/guidelines/docs/ITT_Best_Practices_for_public_statement.pdf.

63 See for the example the "Definitions" in the Annex of the Guidelines for transfers of nuclear-related dual-use, equipment, material, software and related technology of the Nuclear Suppliers Group (available: http://www.nuclearsuppliersgroup.org/Leng/PDF/infcirc254r8p2.pdf), or the Point III of the Related technology of the control list of dual-use chemical manufacturing facilities and equipment and related technology and software of the Australia Group (available: http://www.australiagroup.net/en/dual_chemicals.html).

64 See the definitions provided in the previous chapter.

of natural persons (technical assistance) is not ruled by Regulation 428/2009 but by the Council Joint Action 401/2000, which is a politically binding – and not enforceable – instrument.[65] It allows Member States controlling the transfer of technical assistance when it is provided outside the EU and the exporter is informed or is aware that it is intended for use in connection with the elaboration of a WMD. To implement this control the Member States can establish an obligation to apply for an authorisation or a prohibition to export or a mix of both.[66]

If technologies submitted for control are not necessarily and precisely defined by the international export control instruments, technology not covered is clearly identified through the two exceptions of the public domain and the basic scientific research.

---

[65] Council Joint Action of 22 June 2000 (2000/0401/CFSP) *concerning the control of technical assistance related to certain military end-uses* (*Official Journal* L 159, 30/06/2000, p. 0216-0217).

[66] If most Member States have adopted the authorisation principle, States like Denmark, Italy and Estonia have retained the prohibition principle and Poland and Czech Republic have adopted a mix of both.

The Control Lists

The international control lists

With the development of technologies after the World War II and their potential use in military application, it appeared necessary to control export transactions linked to those technologies, for foreign and security policy considerations. To achieve this goal, it was essential to define a list of materials, equipment and technologies to be submitted for export control. The first lists of items were adopted by the COCOM at the end of the 1950s to counter the risk that Western technologies could be transferred to Warsaw Pact Members States and China. Three lists were adopted and regularly amended through a specific process. The first list included industrial items divided in nine sub-categories,[1] the second was dedicated to conventional arms and their ammunitions and the third concerned the atomic energy and was divided in three sub-categories.[2]

Later, different export control instances dedicated to specific categories of WMD or their means of delivery were created and gave impulse to the adoption of lists of items in connection with chemical or biological weapons. The items listed were called "dual-use" items due to their duality of potential application, both military and peaceful. In principle, the presence of an item in the list subjects it to export authorisation to allow the supplier States assessing that its intended and declared peaceful use would be respected by the final end-user.

The approach retained by the Nuclear Suppliers Group was slightly different since it first listed the items especially designed for nuclear applications, *i.e.* the items that have strictly nuclear applications, without considering if it could or not contribute to the development of nuclear weapons. The discovery of the Iraqi nuclear research programme in early 1990s raised the necessity to extend the list of controlled items to include the dual-use items.

These instances' lists of dual-use items are regularly reviewed and annually updated in order to include the newest technological

---

1 Advanced Materials, Materials Processing, Electronics, Computers, Telecommunications and Information Security, Sensors and Lasers, Navigation and Avionics, Marine, Propulsion.

2 Nuclear Materials, Nuclear Facilities, Nuclear related equipment.

developments and occasionally to decontrol certain out-dated categories.

In the early 1990s, the control by list of items has raised certain concerns. The competition between proliferators to acquire new sensitive technology and State authorities to counter such acquisition by updating the lists of controlled items with new development has not always been in favour of the second ones. The time required for regimes' internal process to achieve the review of its lists might last up to one year and, during this lapse of time, items were not necessarily controlled, which benefited the proliferators. Therefore, the trade control instances have complemented their list-based approach with "catch-all" clauses focusing on the end-use of non-listed items.

Each export control *forum* adopted its lists of items that State parties agreed to submit for authorisation. These lists are organised by categories of items such as "computers", "telecommunication", "plants pathogens", "chemical weapons precursors" or "uranium isotope separation equipment and components". Each category is subdivided in sections like "system", "equipment and components", "material", "software", "technology". The sections contain a certain number of entries describing the different parameters of the controlled items. These descriptions can be completed by technical notes adding information on the items or making links with other sections.

Due to the informal nature of the international export control *fora* and of their non-legally binding guidelines, the lists of controlled items adopted by different regimes have to be transposed by State Parties into their national legislations.

The European control list

Since 1994, the EU compiles in one list the different items listed by the five export control *fora* even if all EU Member States are not necessary members of these instances. The adoption of a common list was necessary to face the single market principle requiring the free movement of the items, including dual-use items, between the 27 Member States.

Each controlled item is labelled with seven digits. The first digit refers to one of the nine categories defined by the Wassenaar Arrangement plus one – category 0 – added to include items controlled by the list of especially-designed nuclear items adopted by the Nuclear Suppliers Group. The second digit (A to E) indicates the potential end-use of the controlled item (*i.e.* "systems", "equipment and components", "test", "inspection and production", "materials", "software" and "technology"). The third digit (0 to 4) defines the international forum which listed the item. The two last digits identify the item itself.

The reference system adopted by the EU is not similar nor compatible with the Harmonised System ("HS code") used by the custom authorities worldwide. Correlation tables were established but their result was rather ineffective, essentially due to the level of specificity used by both systems. The HS reference, indeed, covers all items and not only dual-use items and, even with a higher number of digits, a reference contains more than one item defined by the dual-use list.

The process of implementation of international instances' annual updates and reviews of control items by the EU is lengthy and requires, since the entry into force of the Lisbon Treaty, the approval of both the European Parliament and the Council of Ministers. This process may, therefore, take more than a year.[3]

The United States' control list

The dual-use items controlled by the US Export Administration Regulations are listed in the Commerce Country List (CCL). This list mainly contains dual-use items listed by the international export control *fora* as well as some military items from the Wassenaar Munitions List. The US list is, regarding its structure, similar to the EU list since both implement the same international commitments. Nevertheless, the CCL contains a little less than a third more entries than the EU list. This is due to the maintaining into the CCL of items progressively decontrolled by the regimes in time. It does not necessary mean that the United States control more items than the EU but both systems are not based on the same authorisation requirements. For the EU, an authorisation shall be required to export an item to any destination, whereas, for the US, an item listed could be submitted for authorisation only for certain destinations.

[3] In the future, the European Union may chose to implement a system of "delegated acts", which would allow the European Commission updating the list as soon as the update or review is issued. The subsequent amendments to the EU legislation would be endorsed and "ratified" afterwards by the legislators.

How to Control?

The Authorisations

The controls adapted to the different transactions

The effectiveness of export control regime is strongly dependant on a right choice of transactions to be put under supervision. The *export* transactions were the first type of movements to be controlled under the COCOM. Not surprisingly, the importance of controls of exports can be seen also through the very appellation of the "export control regime".

Currently the four international export control regimes include the export transactions in their scope. Moreover, the controls on exports might be performed according to two specific techniques: the list-based approach and its complement, the catch-all mechanism. Such end-use-based controls, in the context of the catch-all control, constitute a very valuable tool for the licencing authorities. It should however be kept in mind that an excessive use of these provisions may constitute a considerable disadvantage for an economic activity. Therefore, an authorisation will only be required if an exporter was duly informed by a licencing authority (quite often by means of an official letter). Some national or regional regulations[1] may urge an exporter to contact a licencing authority if he is aware or has grounds for suspecting that those items are or may be intended for an end-use of concern.

In addition, there are different ways to limit the exports according to the degree of sensitivity of item (*i.e.* via introduction of specific conditions of use, reporting obligations or end-use guaranties).

It should be noted that States' members of a regional cooperation, as for instance the European Union, might decide to control only exports to third countries. This principle has only one exception, namely Article 22 that provides the rules for restrictions regarding the intra-EU transfers. Accordingly, the transfers of dangerous items listed in Annex IV of Regulation 428/2009 are subject to authorisation.[2] In addition, Article 22(2) enables Member States to impose, under certain conditions an authorisation requirement for the transfer of dual-use items if at the time of transfer, the operator knows that the final destination of the items would be situated outside the EU.

---

1 See Article 4.4 and 4.5 of the Council Regulation 428/2009.

2 This authorisation requirement is not applicable among the Benelux countries.

The *imports* of dual-use items are not usually addressed either by national or by international export control-related provisions. Nevertheless, some States might enact national provisions in order to submit for authorisation certain dual-use items for national public security reasons. An obligation to apply for an import authorisation may sometimes be replaced by a prior notification that might result in an authorisation requirement to be decided by a licencing authority.

The *transit* controls become nowadays more and more challenging. Since early 1990s the international non-proliferation regimes include such controls in their guidelines. The concept of transit might have different interpretations, such as a simple crossing of the territory of State. The notion can also cover the *transhipment* operation-that involves the physical operation of unloading goods from the importing means of transport followed by a reloading onto another exporting means of transport. Generally the restrictive measures will not be applied to every transit operation of dual-use items. The prohibitions or authorisations requirements will be imposed only if there is a risk that the goods in question will or might have an end use of concern (*i.e.* WMD-related end use or a military use in an embargoed country). It should be emphasised that a transit authorisation can be imposed for transaction related to both listed and non-listed items.

Since the adoption in 2004 of Resolution 1540, the *brokering* controls draw the attention of the international community. Therefore, several export control regimes such as the Australia Group and the Wassenaar Arrangement have addressed this issue in their guidelines. Specific provisions on brokering controls are also discussed within the NSG working groups. Similarly to transit, the controls of brokering services would only be applied if there were a certainty or a suspicion that the goods in question will or may have an end-use of concern. A national legislation may go even further and require an authorisation for an activity of brokering in addition to licences for a particular transaction. Moreover, some States maintain national registers of authorised brokers.[3] Eventually, a few national legislations extend brokering controls to nationals that are situated outside the national territory. As for the controls of brokering services as performed by the EU Member States, Article 2(5) of Regulation 428/2009 defines brokering them as "the negotiation or arrangement of transactions for the purchase, sale or supply of dual-use items from a third country to any other third country, or the selling or buying of dual-use items that are located in third countries for their transfer to another third country".

[3] See for instance the Council Common Position 2003/468/CFSP of 23 June 2003 *on the control of arms brokering* (*Official Journal* L 156, 25/6/2003, p. 79).

It is worth mentioning that the auxiliary services such as transportation, financial services, insurance or re-insurance, or general advertising or promotion are not covered by the EU brokering controls. Article 6 of Regulation 428/2009 expressly requires an authorisation for brokering services of dual-use items listed in Annex I if the broker has been informed by his competent authorities that the items for which he proposes brokering services are or may be intended for the WMD-related end use. In case the broker is aware that such use might occur he should inform his competent authorities which will afterwards decide if the transaction should be submitted for authorisation (Article 6.1). Moreover, the optional controls were laid down in Article 6.2 for:

- The brokering services of non-listed dual-use items intended for WMD-related end-use;
- The brokering services of both listed and non-listed dual-use items intended for military end-use in embargoed countries; and
- The brokering services of non-listed dual-use items if the broker has grounds for suspecting potential WMD end-use.

The latest technological achievements have made it clear that the *transfers of technology* should also be encompassed into the scope of export controls. Several export control regimes either have developed the specific guidelines related to intangible transfers or have established the same types of control for the dual-use items and related technology. The Wassenaar Arrangement for instance has adopted in 2006 the Best Practices For Implementing Intangible Transfer of Technology Controls.[4] This document invites the State Parties to lay down the national laws and regulations with clear definitions of ITT via both oral and electronic means of transmission. Taking into account the difficulties linked to the practical implementation of ITT controls, the Wassenaar guidelines emphasise the importance of self-regulation initiatives to be taken by the industry and the academic institutions. In particular they refer to the implementation of internal compliance programmes as well as stressing the need of continuous industry outreach and awareness raising related to the ITT controls. The MTCR, NSG and Australia Group foresee the same type of controls for both tangible and intangible transfers. The general principles of ITT controls are the following: they usually do not apply to information in the *public domain* or to *basic scientific research*; the transmission of software or technology via *electronic means*, such as fax, telephone, electronic mail is controlled, whereas the ITT that involve *cross-border movement of*

4 For the Best Practices For Implementing Intangible Transfer of Technology Controls, see: http://www.wassenaar.org/guidelines/docs/ITT_Best_Practices_for_public_statement.pdf.

persons are usually left outside the scope of the controls foreseen by the international guidelines.

The different types of authorisations

Even if the dual-use items might have an end-use of concern, it should be kept in mind that their first object remains civil. Therefore, the legislators, together with the licencing authorities, should find the right balance between the legitimate trade and the non-proliferation requirement. The adjustments of types of authorisations might indeed be one of the possible ways for developing the equilibrium between these somewhat opposite concepts. This need for further flexibility may be the main explanation why the provisions on types of authorisations are missing in the international export instances' guidelines.

The latitude of an authorisation is determined according to a number and nature of potential recipients and countries of destination along with an end-use.

The individual authorisation

The most restrictive type of authorisation is the individual authorisation, which enables the exporter to deliver a *specific quantity* of dual-use items to a *specific end-user* situated in a *specific country*. It should however be emphasised that in case the delivery is carried on through several physical transactions, they would still be covered by a unique individual authorisation.

These "one shot" authorisations are in particular used for the transactions that involve especially sensitive elements such as destination, end-user, end-use, etc. Generally speaking, all necessary end-user or end-use controls are accomplished by a licencing authority before the granting of an individual authorisation. The validity of an authorisation typically varies from one to two years. When a licence is either expired or used it should be returned to a licencing authority, provided that it was cleared by the customs. If a licence has expired but the entire delivery did not take place, a licence might be renewed even though this procedure does not occur automatically. A renewal of a licence constitutes a new administrative decision and a licencing authority might refuse to renew a licence in the case it considers that there is any concern related to the whole transaction.

The global authorisation

The global authorisation (sometimes referred to as an "open authorisation") offers more freedom to the exporters, given that it authorises exports of a number of *different types of dual-use items* to be exported to *different recipients* situated in *different countries* of destination.

The period of validity is generally longer than that of an individual authorisation but there is no rule. Moreover, besides the prior controls, the granting of a global authorisation may be subject to or facilitated by the implementation by an exporter of an internal compliance programme.

The use of global export authorisations becomes more and more frequent worldwide. This type of authorisation, indeed, constitutes a flexible instrument that allows for meeting the needs of exporters in the current globalised economy.

The general authorisation

The least restrictive type of authorisation is the general export authorisation. This authorisation might be used by *all national exporters* that meet the conditions of use and allows them to export *several types of dual-use items* to *several recipients* situated in *pre-determined countries* of destination.

The general export authorisations are usually adopted at the national level and, therefore, constitute a valuable instrument to stimulate the national economy. A specific general export authorisation may therefore be enacted for a specific commercial project or international cooperation. The use of general licences is conditioned upon a *prior registration* and specific *reporting* and *record-keeping* requirements.

In the case of the European Union, the dual-use Regulation provides a legal basis for the enactment of the national general export authorisations (NGEA), provided that they meet a set of requirements. According to Article 9.4 an NGEA should not be in conflict with the EUGEA and the scope of an NGEA should not include the items listed in Annex II(g) of the Regulation. The NGEA are notified to the Commission that assures the publication thereof in the C series of the Official Journal of the European Union.[5]

Moreover, the general export authorisations can be adopted directly at the EU level. According to the Article 2.9 of the Regulation, the "Union general export authorisation shall mean an export authorisation for exports to certain countries of destination available to all exporters

---

[5] Several EU Member States have enacted a number of NGEA. For more information on the NGEA adopted by the EU Member States on national basis, see Michel, Q., "The European Union Dual-Use Items Control Regime: Comment of the Legislation: article-by-article", available at: http://local.droit.ulg.ac.be/jcms/service/index.php?serv=49&cat=3.

who respect its conditions of use". With the adoption of Regulation 1232/2011 the European Union enacted six EUGEA:[6]

- EU001: exports to Australia, Canada, Japan, New Zealand, Norway, Switzerland (including Liechtenstein) and United States of America;
- EU002: export of certain dual-use items to certain destinations;
- EU003: export after repair/replacement;
- EU004: temporary export for exhibition or fair;
- EU005: telecommunications;
- EU006: chemicals.

Whereas the EUGEA are directly granted by the European Union, they still need a further implementation by the 27 Member States. The basic implementing steps include setting the rules concerning the notification procedure, reporting requirement (*i.e.* annually, monthly, on request) and record-keeping obligation. A licencing authority may prevent the exporter from using an EUGEA if there is reasonable suspicion about its ability to comply with such authorisation or with a provision of the export control legislation.[7]

The US legislation also contains a specific export-facilitating instrument which largely resembles a general licence. A strategic trade authorisation (STA) allows the exports, re-exports or in-country transfers to *specific countries without a licence*. The countries of destination are assessed as having a lower risk of illegal end-use or diversion. The items concerned are the items otherwise controlled for the following reasons: regional stability, national security, nuclear non-proliferation, chemical and biological weapons and crime control. The STA are used on voluntary basis and are subject to a registration, prior consignee statement and recordkeeping requirement.

The information and documents required

A set of additional documents to be submitted together with the licence application form varies according to the national legislation of each country. As a rule the applicant should provide the competent authorities with "all necessary documents" to identify the focal elements of the transaction:

6 *Official Journal* L 326, 8/12/2011, p. 26.

7 See Article 9.1 of the Regulation 428/2009 as amended by the Regulation 1232/2011.

- The exporter;
- The description of the goods;
- The country of origin;
- The country of destination;
- The end-user;
- If applicable, the consignee;
- The end use;
- The end use location.

In most cases, the exporter is asked to submit an end-user certificate (EUC) filled up and signed by his commercial partner. The competent authorities might need some additional end-use or end-user assurances and require the mention of a no re-export clause and/or the WMD-clause.

Although there is no commonly accepted EUC template the European Union, in 2008, has adopted the "Best practice recommendations for elements of a Community End-Use Certificate".[8] Agreed by the Council Working Party on Dual-Use Goods, this document establishes that the EUC shall mention the following fields:

- The parties: exporter, consignee, end-user, country of destination;
- The items: description, end-use, end-use location, quantity and weight;
- The additional guaranties: non-proliferation clause, no re-export clause (optional).

This document should be issued on a letterhead paper of the end-user or consignee in the country of the final destination. If issued by the government authority, the EUC should contain a unique identifying certificate number. These recommendations are not legally binding. Nevertheless, the Member States globally follow the main principles of this document. Moreover, some States insist on the fact that the EUC should be certified, for example, by a Chamber of Commerce situated in the country of destination or another relevant authority.

A licencing authority may also make a delivery of a licence to condition upon the issuance of an international import certificate (IIC) and/or a delivery verification certificate (DVC) issued by the competent authorities of the importing State.

---

[8] For the "Best practice recommendations for elements of a Community End-Use Certificate", see: http://trade.ec.europa.eu/doclib/docs/2009/june/tradoc_143395.en08.pdf.

These documents are to assure that the import will not be diverted, transhipped, re-exported, or otherwise transferred to another destination except in compliance with the export control legislation of the importing State.

More Controls, More Assurances

The catch-all clauses

In order to address a rapid progression of technology as well as to circumvent the proliferators' endeavours to procure the dual-use items with technical specifications just below the controlled ones, the export control requirements might, under some circumstances, be extended in order to include non-listed dual-use items.

Such additional controls should however be put in practice with a lot of caution considering that they afford the licencing authority an opportunity to control a wide range of essentially civil goods. Therefore, the so-called catch-all mechanisms cover only a very limited number of hypotheses related, in particular, to an end-use of concern. The transactions relating to non-listed dual-use items might indeed be subject to authorisation if the items in question are or may be intended in their entirety or in part, for a WMD-related end-use, or for a military end-use in embargoed countries.

Practically, an exporter will usually be *informed* of the end-use of concern by the national licencing authority (also referred to as the "level 1" catch-all) and consequently will be entitled to submit a licence application. Moreover, an authorisation requirement might be broadened to include the event when an exporter is *aware of* ("level 2") or has *reasons for suspecting* ("level 3") a sensitive end-use. He should inform the competent authority, which will further decide if an authorisation is necessary.

A catch-all provision is provided for most international export control regimes. As for the Australia Group, Article 1 urges Participating States to require an authorisation for the transfer of non-listed items where the exporter is aware or is informed by the competent authorities of the Participant State in which it is established that the items in question may be intended, in their entirety or part, for use in connection with chemical or biological weapons activities. The MTCR guidelines address in Point 7 an authorisation requirement for the transfer of non-listed items if the exporter is aware or has been informed by the competent authorities of the Government that the items may be intended, in their entirety or part, for use in connection with delivery systems for weapons of mass destruction other than manned aircraft. A Statement of Understanding on Control of Non-Listed Dual-Use Items adopted within the framework of the Wassenaar Arrangement contains a similar provision regarding the transfers of items that are or may be intended, entirely or in part, for a military end-use.

The no re-export clause

The "no re-export" clause shall be regarded as an additional assurance that prohibits a subsequent export without the prior authorisation of the exporting State or that totally bans any further re-export. The no re-export clause has progressively become one of the focal points related to the provision of the end-use guarantees.

In function of the sensitivity of the end-user, end-use or country of destination, the extent of the no re-export clause may differ considerably. In the event of a very sensitive transaction a full ban on any re-export is generally envisaged. A sensitive transaction may necessitate the prior consent of the competent authorities of the exporting State. Finally the least sensitive transactions are usually associated with the prior consent of the competent authorities of the importing State.

The no re-export clause is explicitly provided for by all four international export control regimes:

- The Australia Group guidelines, Point 5;[1]
- The MTCR guidelines, Point 5.B;[2]
- The NSG guidelines, Point 7;[3]
- The Wassenaar Arrangement "Best Practice Guidelines on Subsequent Transfer (Re-export) Controls for Conventional Weapons Systems" contained in Appendix 3 to the WA Initial Elements.[4]

As regards the Member States of the European Union, a non-binding model for an end-user certificate – presented above – lays down two optional provisions on further re-export restrictions. In case a *consignee acts as end-user*, it shall certify that it would not re-export the items to third countries without the consent of a competent body to be determined (*i.e.* the licencing authority of the supplier State or that of a recipient State). If a *consignee acts as trader*, it shall declare that the

1 For the Australia Group guidelines, see: http://www.australiagroup.net/en/guidelines.html.

2 For the MTCR guidelines, see: http://www.mtcr.info/english/guidetext.htm.

3 For the NSG guidelines, see: http://www.nuclearsuppliersgroup.org/Leng/PDF/infcirc254r8p2.pdf.

4 For the WA "Best Practice" guidelines, see: http://www.wassenaar.org/guidelines/docs/3%20-%20Re-export.pdf.

customer will not re-export the goods to third countries without the consent of the competent body to be determined. Although the no re-export clause is compulsory under the EU guidelines, it leaves the Member States with lots of room to manoeuvre as regards the practical implementation thereof, in particular in terms of the extension of a re-export ban.

The non-proliferation clause

The non-proliferation clause is another end-use guarantee. Even if the scope of this clause may differ, the present trends require it to be as explicit as possible, especially as regards the prohibited end-use. The non-proliferation clause specifies that the exported items will only be used for the *declared purposes* and will not be utilised in any nuclear explosive activity or unsafeguarded nuclear fuel-cycle activity, nor will they be used for any purpose connected with chemical or biological or nuclear weapons, or missiles capable of delivering such weapons.

The EU model for the end-user certificate contains the mention of a non-proliferation clause that differs according to the role of consignee. If *consignee acts as end-user* it would have to certify that the items would be exclusively used for the declared purposes and under no circumstances whatsoever will be used for WMD programmes. If the *consignee acts as trader, whole- or re-seller*, they would have to provide a similar statement on behalf of their customer and be considered absolutely reliable.

The no-undercut principle

The "no-undercut" principle constitutes the cornerstone of every regional or international export control agreement. It is absolutely indispensable for the effectiveness of a multilateral cooperation because it contributes to the elimination of a "licence shopping" and provides a more equal level-playing field. The no-undercut principle commits a State party of an export control cooperation to consult, before granting an authorisation, another State party that has already denied an *essentially identical* transaction. Even if the results of such consultation are not legally binding, there is often a political pressure that may force the State parties to follow the same line of action. Nevertheless, if a State party decides to grant the licence it shall so inform all other members of the export control cooperation.

The concept of "essentially identical" transaction remains undefined by the majority of the international export control instances. The definition thereof is however provided by the Article 13.5 of the European dual-use Regulation, according to which an essentially identical transaction should mean "an item with essentially identical parameters or technical characteristics to the same end user or consignee".

An explicit no-undercut provision is only provided for by the Australia Group guidelines.[5] As for the Wassenaar Arrangement, although it does not establish a genuine no-undercut principle, it urges the State Parties to notify the others of a licence approval for an essentially identical transaction previously denied by another State Party.[6]

---

5 In accordance with the Group's agreed procedures, a licence for an export that is essentially identical to one denied by another AG participant will only be granted after consultations with that participant, provided it has not expired or been rescinded. Essentially identical is defined as being the same biological agent or chemical or, in the case of dual-use equipment, equipment which has the same or similar specifications and performance being sold to the same consignee. The terms of the Group's "no-undercut policy" do not apply to denials of items under national catch-all provisions.

6 In accordance with the provisions of this Arrangement, the Participating States agree to notify the transfers and denials. These notifications will apply to all non-participating States. However, in the light of the general and specific information exchange, the scope of these notifications, as well as their relevance for the purposes of the Arrangement, will be reviewed. The notification of a denial will not impose an obligation on other Participating States to deny similar transfers. However, a Participating State will notify, preferably within 30 days, but no later than within 60 days, all other Participating States of an approval of a licence which has been denied by another Participating State for an essentially identical transaction during the last three years. See the WA Initial Elements, Part II.4.

The Elements of a Licencing Procedure

The elements to be checked by the applicant

The controlled items are generally contained in specific national and/or international control lists, notwithstanding the potential application of catch-all clauses. The *rating* – or decision about whether or not the technical parameters of an item are equal to those specified by the control lists – is a primary responsibility of the exporter. It is therefore highly recommended to possess a sufficient technical expertise in order to duly perform this task. In order to do so, an exporter may in addition use several specific online tools,[1] or ask the licencing authority or a specialised body for a rating assistance.

Given that an exporter has presumably a privileged knowledge of its clients, they will be asked to provide the most *extensive information* about both the end-user and the end-use. The plausibility of this information will be further crosschecked by the competent authorities throughout the various inter-agency and international cooperation channels. It should be noted that more thorough checks might be undertaken if a transaction is destined to a local distributor instead of the end-user of an item. Moreover, a further check of trustworthiness of the end-use would have to be undertaken in order to exclude any possibility of WMD-related end-use or illegal military end-use. The licencing authority may ask for additional guaranties to be provided by a consignee, such as an end-user certificate, an international import certificate or a delivery verification certificate.

A *country of destination* constitutes significant and often crucial data in the course of assessment of a licence application. A peculiarity of a country of destination might cardinally influence the whole dossier. Sometimes a transaction is blocked when a country of destination is, for example, subject to an embargo. On the contrary, it might not require any authorisation at all if the country fits the conditions for example of an EU general licence or an American strategic trade authorisation. Some countries, such as the United States, literally base their national export control policies on considerations related to a country of

---

1 Such as the British software *Goods Checker*. For more information, see: http://www.ecochecker.bis.gov.uk/.

destination.[2] Various US authorities competent for the strategic trade controls publish a number of different watch lists related to sensitive end-users:

- The Denied Persons List;[3]
- The Entity List;[4]
- The Unverified List.[5]

As for the European Union as a whole, it publishes a comprehensive list of the embargoed countries that includes both the UNSC and EU specific embargoes. This list provides extensive country-based information and includes further details regarding the scope of embargoes and links to the relevant legal provisions.[6] As regards the EU Member States, only the United Kingdom has enacted a specific Iranian List,[7] which constitutes a watch list.

The customs clearance

After receiving an export authorisation from a national licencing authority, the exporter is entitled to present the items to the customs office. In some countries the handling of the export declaration for dual-use items may be conducted only by specific customs offices.[8]

The exporter is therefore invited to fulfil the necessary customs formalities. If the accompanying documents are in order the custom officer will clear a licence by decreasing the quantity of goods authorised for export by the number of goods being currently exported. Consequently an export licence is generally subject to several clearance operations, notably in the event of global authorisations.

---

2 A prior licence requirement might be checked by an exporter though a so-called Country Chart, which represents a double-entry table which links a country of destination with a possible reason of export control. About the Country Chart, see: http://www.ecfr.gov/cgi-bin/text-idx?c=ecfr&sid=59ee1d5eeb8f1d444ba88927fa1eaaff&rgn=div9&view=text&node=15:2.1.3.4.24.0.1.5.27&idno=15.

3 See: http://www.bis.doc.gov/dpl/default.shtm.

4 See: http://www.bis.doc.gov/entities/default.htm.

5 See: http://www.bis.doc.gov/enforcement/unverifiedlist/unverified_parties.html.

6 For more information on the EU restrictive measures in force, see: http://eeas.europa.eu/cfsp/sanctions/docs/measures_en.pdf.

7 For more information on the Iran List, see: https://www.gov.uk/iran-list-wmd-end-use-control.

8 See for example: Article 17 of the Regulation 428/2009.

The end-user and end-use post-shipment verifications

Only the NSG and the CWC have adopted provisions related to the post-shipment's end-use or end-user verifications. If, for the CWC, its technical secretariat is assigned this task, the NSG does not establish any specific structure and delegates the verification to the IAEA. At the national level, some States may require a *delivery verification certificate* which confirms that the items have been effectively delivered but does not guarantee that the declared end-use will be respected or that the items will not be re-exported afterwards.

Within the framework of the NSG

The export of nuclear-related dual-use items can be authorised by the NSG only if the recipient State has brought into force an agreement with the IAEA requiring an application of *safeguards* on all sources and special fissionable material in its current and future peaceful activities.[9] The NSG safeguards requirement is backed up by several provisions organising either the restitution of the items or the safeguards to be applied, in case the agreement with the IAEA would be terminated. This also applies if the Agency decides that the application of safeguards is no longer possible. The IAEA does not interact directly with the NSG. Any breach of end-user's safeguards obligations found by the inspection team are reported to the IAEA Board of Governors which may decide to submit the case to the UN Security Council. Although the Agency does not have a formal link with the NSG, several actions taken by the Agency constrain the export policy applied by the NSG Member States. The export of enrichment or reprocessing facilities, equipment or technology, for example shall not be authorised if the recipient has been identified by the Agency as being in breach to comply with its safeguards obligations or if the Agency is unable to implement its safeguards agreement.[10]

Within the framework of the CWC

The verification mechanism established by the CWC mandates its Technical Secretariat to control that listed chemicals are being used solely for permitted purposes. Three types of *inspections* or investigations are foreseen under the Convention:

- The *routine inspections* are conducted at declared industrial facilities that produce, process or, in certain cases, consume the

---

9 IAEA, INFCIRC/253/Rev.10/Part.1, Guidelines for Nuclear Transfers, July 2011, Paragraph 4.

10 *Idem*, Paragraph 6.

listed chemicals. These inspections are designed to verify, on the one hand, the accuracy of information declared by State Parties in their initial and annual declarations, and, on the other hand, that the activities of the State Parties are in accordance with the Convention.

- The *challenge inspections* are provided for under the Convention, which grants to each State Party the right to request the Director-General to undertake at short notice an OPCW inspection on the territory of any State Party, or at any location under the jurisdiction or control of any other State Party, in order to clarify and resolve any questions of possible non-compliance.
- The *investigation of alleged use* can be conducted by the OPCW at the request of a State Party, either to confirm the actual use or threat of use of chemical weapons, or to assess the need for assistance, or both.

This specific verification system attached to the CWC pursues the same objective as the one established by the IAEA, even if it is not linked to the UNSC.

The submission for a verification mechanism does not constitute a condition of supply for the Australia Group even if the applicability of relevant multilateral agreements, including the CWC, is a factor to consider when assessing an export application.[11]

The cooperation with the industry

The internal compliance programmes (ICP)

The effective countering of the WMD proliferation is nowadays hardly conceivable without the involvement of the industrial sector. By definition, an exporter should know his or her client and therefore can furnish a licencing authority with valuable information. Consequently, according to current trends in export control the predominant approach would be to offer wider export facilities to the economic operators that provide a number of guarantees in terms of compliance. The implementation of an internal compliance programme by an exporter within its organisation is the sign of the due share of responsibility and liability the private sector is willing to take in the non-proliferation effort.

The decision to put in practice an ICP shall result from a thorough assessment of a number of factors such as:

---

11 Australia Group "Guidelines for Transfers of Sensitive Chemical or Biological Items", Paragraph 4.g.

- The size of the organisation;
- The end-use and sensitivity of products;
- The geographic location of the business and customers;
- The relationships with the business partners;
- The volume of exports;
- The product restriction; and
- The complexity of internal export processes.[12]

Moreover, these factors will influence the extent to which an ICP will be implemented. An effective ICP should, indeed, at least comprise the following measures:

- A commitment, which should be endorsed by a senior executive, to comply with the relevant export control regulations;
- A centralised export control management;
- A continuous update as regards the national and international export control legislation;
- The training of the concerned employees;
- The effective screening of the inquiries and, if applicable, alerting (*i.e.* country of destination, end-user, consignee, end-use, etc.);
- The development of relevant export control documentation (*i.e.* record-keeping, annual reports, etc.);
- Continuous audits.

It should be kept in mind that, for the time being, an ICP does not constitute a generally applicable requirement that might give grounds for claiming any export facilitation. However a suitable implementation of an ICP will most likely result in a *favourable treatment* by a licencing authority. Such an approach seems indeed to constitute an appropriate balance between the boost of the economic activity and the countering of the WMD proliferation. Although any export control regime requires an ICP as a condition of supply, in 2011 the Wassenaar Arrangement had issued a set of comprehensive guidelines on ICP for dual-use goods and technologies.[13]

---

12 See "Compliance Guidelines: How to Develop an Effective Export Management and Compliance Program and Manual", US Department of Commerce, Bureau of Industry and Security, p. 3, available at http://www.bis.doc.gov/complianceandenforcement/emcp_guidelines.pdf.

13 For the Wassenaar Arrangement "Best Practice Guidelines on Internal Compliance Programmes for Dual-Use Goods and Technologies", see: http://www.wassenaar.org/guidelines/docs/2%20-%20Internal%20Compliance%20Programmes.pdf.

As for the EU, according to Article 12.2 of the dual-use Regulation, while assessing a *global export licence* application the competent authorities should take into consideration the application by the exporter of proportionate and adequate means and procedures to ensure compliance with the provisions and objectives of the relevant export control legislation, which clearly makes a link to the ICP. Moreover, with regard to the defence-related products, being the goods that appear on the EU Military List,[14] the EU legislator has introduced a specific general licence for the intra-EU transfers destined for the certified undertakings. A related certification procedure is largely inspired by and based on an ICP. Consequently, an ICP becomes a real facilitator at least as it concerns the movements of military items within the EU.

In Japan, although not compulsory for all the different licences, the implementation of an ICP is strongly encouraged by the authority. A list of undertakings registered as having implemented an ICP, and therefore considered as reliable, is available on the website of the Ministry of Economy, Trade and Industry.[15]

The information sharing through outreach and training

Taking into account the greater involvement of the economic operators in present export control mechanisms, it becomes essential for a licencing authority to assure proper *information exchange*.

Such exchange, which varies according to the nature and extent of the relation between the authorities and the private sector, can concern at least the following subjects:

- The updates in export control legislation (national, regional, international);
- The latest restrictive measures;
- The changes in the control lists;
- The communications related to the application of catch-all clauses;
- The various watch lists (*e.g.* end-users, countries of destination, items).

This exchange can take different forms, such as a newsletter, an update of a website of a licencing authority, a communication via specific channels (*i.e.* chambers of commerce or industry associations).

---

14 For the current version of the Common Military List of the European Union, see: http://eur-lex.europa.eu/LexUriServ/LexUriServ.do?uri=OJ:C:2012:085:0001:0036:EN:PDF.

15 CISTEC, “Overview of Japan’s Export Controls”, Third edition, October 2012, p. 34.

A licencing authority may also undertake a series of *outreach* activities either at the request of economic operators or at its own initiative. These activities are usually envisaged as regular tutorials or training on the export control fundamentals or as special seminars dedicated to a specific issue, such as a new regulation in force, a public consultation, etc. In principle, the information related to the outreach activities and trainings organised by the national licencing authorities is public and made available on their websites. The economic operators as well as academia are accordingly invited to check and update them consistently.

The status of authorised economic operator (AEO)

The concept of authorised economic operator was initially developed under the aegis of the World Customs Organisation. The basic principle of an AEO certification is that an economic operator shall implement a number of procedures aimed at securing his supply chain as well as assuring an appropriate monitoring of its record keeping and reporting obligations. The national customs authorities shall then analyse these internal adjustments and, if they approve them, the economic operator in question will obtain an AEO status that entails simplified customs proceedings as, for instance, a faster clearance procedure or a reduction of the number of inspections.

Within the EU, the AEO policy was inaugurated in 2005 in order to provide facilitations for the customs controls with regard to security, safety and for the customs rules simplifications.[16] The EU introduces the same standards for the European industries wishing to benefit from the customs simplifications. The status, therefore, contributes to the creation of a more balanced and level-playing field within the EU. According to the EU legislation, the criteria for granting the status of an authorised economic operator includes:

- An appropriate record of compliance with customs requirements;
- A satisfactory system of managing commercial and, where appropriate, transport records, which allows appropriate customs controls;
- Where appropriate, proven financial solvency; and
- Where applicable, appropriate security and safety standards.[17]

---

16 Regulation (EC) No. 648/2005 of the European Parliament and of the Council of 13 April 2005 amending Council Regulation (EEC) No. 2913/92 *establishing the Community Customs Code* (*Official Journal* L 117, 04/05/2005, p. 13), Article 5a.

17 Ibid. More detailed provisions were laid down by the Commission Regulation (EC) No. 1875/2006 of 18 December 2006 amending Regulation (EEC) No. 2454/93 laying down provisions for the implementation of Council Regulation (EEC) No.

Currently there are three different AEO statuses available for the European exporters:

- The *AEO-Customs simplifications*, which establishes diverse simplifications specifically provided for under the customs legislation;
- The *AEO-Security and safety*, which establishes particular facilitations related to customs controls concerning security and safety when the goods enter or leave the customs territory of the EU;
- The *AEO-Customs simplifications/security and safety*, which establishes diverse simplifications specifically provided for under the customs legislation and from particular facilitations related to customs controls concerning security and safety.[18]

The European Commission maintains an online database of the certified AEO who agreed that their details could be published.[19] The status of AEO granted by one Member State is valid throughout the European Union. Such AEO, however, does not get automatic access to customs simplifications laid down by the other Member States.

In order to assist the economic operators in learning and understanding the relevant legislation applicable to the AEO as well as the procedure to become an AEO, the Commission has developed a specific course, which is free and is available online.[20]

Nevertheless, for the time being, an AEO status only entails different simplifications specifically provided for under the customs legislation along with the facilitations related to specific customs controls. There exists no connection with the licencing procedure, *per se*.

2913/92 *establishing the Community Customs Code* (*Official Journal* L 360, 19/12/2006, p. 64).

18 For more information regarding the various AEO status and related criteria for granting, see the "AEO Guidelines", available: http://ec.europa.eu/taxation_customs/resources/documents/customs/policy_issues/customs_security/aeo_guidelines2012_en.pdf.

19 In order to consult the Economic Operator System, see: http://ec.europa.eu/taxation_customs/dds2/eos/eos_home.jsp?Lang=en.

20 The AEO e-learning tool is available at the following address: http://ec.europa.eu/taxation_customs/common/elearning/aeo/index_en.htm.

Non-proliferation & security

The aim of this book series is to study the various aspects of risk linked to human activities.

Scientific and technological development is changing our society fundamentally and the concept of risk is crucial for the analysis of the ongoing social transformation process.

Progress in genetic engineering and the use of military technology by civilians, for instance, raise questions concerning ethical, political, environmental and public-health issues.

This series, therefore, opts for a multidisciplinary approach to the problem of risk, which involves the scientific community as much as the political world and civil society.

It publishes monographs and collected papers, mainly in French or English.

Series editors: Quentin MICHEL & Sébastien BRUNET,
Université de Liège (Belgium)

Published Books

N° 9 – Quentin MICHEL, Sylvain PAILE, Maryna TSUKANOVA, Andrea VISKI, *Controlling the Trade of the Dual-Use Items. A Handbook*, 2013.

N° 8 – Odette JANKOWITSCH-PREVOR, Quentin MICHEL (eds.), *European Dual-Use Trade Controls. Beyond Materiality and Borders*, 2013.

N° 7 – André DUMOULIN, Delphine DESCHAUX-BEAUME et Sylvain PAILE (dir.), *Politiques de communication, médias et défense. L'OTAN et la PSDC : visibilité en Belgique et chez ses voisins*, 2013.

N° 6 – Quentin MICHEL, *Concilier l'inconciliable. Les régimes internationaux et européens de contrôle du commerce nucléaire*, 2012

N° 5 – Quentin MICHEL (ed.), *Sensitive Trade. The Perspective of European States*, 2011

N° 4 – Quentin MICHEL (ed.), *Terrorisme. Regards croisés / Terrorism. Cross Analysis*, 2005

N° 3 – Sébastien BRUNET, Anne BERGMANS, Anne BERTRAND & Patrick BIREN (dir.), *L'expertise en questions. Domestiquer l'incertitude dans la société du risque*, 2002

N° 2 – Pierre HUPET (dir.), *Risque et systèmes complexes. Les enjeux de la communication*, 2001

N° 1 – CD-Rom, Quentin MICHEL, *Articles nucléaires et articles à double usage : régulation du commerce au sein de l'Union européenne. Doctrine, jurisprudence et législation*, 2001.

www.peterlang.com

FSC
www.fsc.org
MIX
Papier | Fördert
gute Waldnutzung
FSC® C083411

Kolibri 360 GmbH
Ferdinand-Jühlke-Straße 7
99095 Erfurt, Deutschland
produktsicherheit@kolibri360.de